THE STREET-SMART PARABLES

The Small Book With Profound Insights!

THE STREET-SMART PARABLES

The Small Book With Profound Insights!

IN WORK AND IN LIFE
ONLY THE STREET-SMART SURVIVE

J.R. STERLING

JAICO PUBLISHING HOUSE
Ahmedabad Bangalore Bhopal Bhubaneswar Chennai
Delhi Hyderabad Kolkata Lucknow Mumbai

Published by Jaico Publishing House
A-2 Jash Chambers, 7-A Sir Phirozshah Mehta Road
Fort, Mumbai - 400 001
jaicopub@jaicobooks.com
www.jaicobooks.com

© J. R. Sterling

THE STREET-SMART PARABLES
ISBN 81-7992-344-4

First Jaico Impression: 2006

No part of this book may be reproduced or utilized in
any form or by any means, electronic or
mechanical including photocopying, recording or by any
information storage and retrieval system,
without permission in writing from the publishers.

Dedicated

To my grand parents, parents and brother

Contents

	A Gathering	ix
1.	The Sport	1
	The Sport – A Discussion	9
2.	The Temple	13
	The Temple – A Discussion	19
3.	Almarado's Horse	22
	Almarado's Horse – A Discussion	28
4.	Damsels In Distress	30
	Damsels In Distress – A Discussion	38
5.	The Fortress	41
	The Fortress – A Discussion	45
6.	The Bells	47
	The Bells – A Discussion	52
7.	The Dragon Slayer	54
	The Dragon Slayer – A Discussion	59
8.	Once I Was A Prince	61
	Once I Was A Prince – A Discussion	64
9.	The Five Guardians	67
	The Five Guardians – A Discussion	78

Contents

10.	The White Elephant	80
	The White Elephant – A Discussion	85
11.	The Two Princes	87
	The Two Princes – A Discussion	96
12.	The Dramatist	98
	The Dramatist – A Discussion	106
13.	The Knight And The Farmer	108
	The Knight And The Farmer – A Discussion	120
14.	A War Averted	122
	A War Averted – A Discussion	126

A Gathering

One Sunday, three former classmates gathered for lunch. In high school, they had been the thickest of friends and continued to be so with the passage of every year. At least once in a year, they would gather in one of their homes and discuss about what was happening in each other's lives. After lunch, they got down to the 'business' of discussing what was happening in their lives.

Richard, who had started his own business, was delighted to discuss how his business had done extremely well that year. He expected a double digit growth the next year.

Anne, who had been promoted as a Manager in the company she was employed, explained how the new responsibility had brought greater challenges in her work. She had already achieved some of her targets and was confident of achieving the remaining.

They, then, turned their attention to Sterling, who was his usual quiet self.

'So, Sterling, what is your latest project?' Anne asked.

Sterling was a management consultant and researcher.

'Well, I have completed my first book,' Sterling said. 'It is titled 'The Street-Smart Parables'.'

'The Street Smart Parables?' Anne asked 'What is it about?'

'It is a collection of fourteen parables,' Sterling said. 'Each is a simple story which conveys practical wisdom. That is why I have titled it as 'Street-Smart'.'

'Hey! Why don't you read out the stories to us?' Anne asked

'And we can have a discussion after each story is read out.' Richard said.

'Great!' said Sterling and then began to read out his first story..................

1 | The Sport

The Emperor woke up from his reverie. The spectators in the amphitheatre were cheering hysterically. The fight between the two gladiators had almost come to an end and the victor was asking the Emperor whether he should kill the vanquished or spare his life.

The Emperor got up from his seat. The spectators and the gladiators held their breath.

Will the Emperor's thumb go up or down? They asked themselves.

Every thumb in the amphitheatre had gone down but the Emperor pointed his thumb upwards; he was happy to spare one more life. Ever since he had become the Emperor; he had been sparing lives whenever he could.

Some of the spectators sighed in despair while others groaned in disapproval. Once again the Emperor had cheated them of their fun.

The spectators were disgruntled because it was not sufficient for them just to see blood spill; their entertainment would not be complete unless the fight climaxed in the victor chopping off the head of the vanquished. The victorious gladiator was disappointed, as he could not consummate his victory by killing his opponent. Only the defeated gladiator was greatly relieved and thankful, as the Emperor had saved him from certain death.

The Emperor could not assimilate how the citizens could enjoy such a savage sport-two persons were fighting like beasts unto death! He also knew that they bet heavily that their favourite gladiator would win. So when heads rolled or limbs were severed, there would be some spectators who would be depressed, not because they were in any way moved by the gory sight they witnessed, but since they had lost their wagers.

The spectacle of a wretched criminal being thrown to a hungry lion was even harder for him to stomach As the beast ripped off the hapless convict, the amphitheatre would drown in the din of blood hungry cries .Only he turned his head away in anguish. Even if the criminal deserved to die, he didn't deserve such an excruciating death.

Someone had to put an end to all this repugnant madness.

The citizens were finding it increasingly difficult to put up with the Emperor. Here was an Emperor who would spare a life if he could. He was more comfortable with playing the harp than wielding the sword. The awesome army had been hardly engaged in any war of significance and the soldiers were restless. He seemed to be uninterested in the Games but at the same time seemed to be obsessed with arts and literature. And he had not inherited the greatness of his illustrious predecessors, if greatness was to be measured in terms of wars won, cities destroyed, civilians killed and monuments built.

But one man was immensely pleased with how things were shaping up – he was General Telemachus.

Telemachus coveted the throne and he was waiting for the right opportunity to strike.

Now that discontent was simmering against the Emperor, he felt he stood a favourable chance of usurping power. With this ulterior motive, he and his sycophants began to spread slander against the Emperor and elicit tacit support from the Senators.

One day, when the spectators were waiting impatiently for the gladiator sports to begin, the Emperor made a dramatic announcement:

'Henceforth there shall not be any entertainment involving violence of any kind. Hence I am abolishing gladiator sports. No criminal will henceforth be thrown mercilessly to the lions; if they deserve to die, they will die a more peaceful death. I will not allow blood to be spilled in this amphitheatre.'

The spectators greeted the announcement with shocked disbelief and silence.

'From today,' the Emperor continued, 'we shall have operas and plays. The great dramatist, Edius will present his drama today.'

There were murmurs of protest.

Edius began to present his drama. The Emperor thought it was a great drama but however great it was it could not measure up to the real-life drama that the audience had been accustomed to. By the time the play was over, most of the spectators had left.

The amphitheatre began to wear a deserted look; only a select few who could appreciate arts frequented it and the only regular patron was the Emperor.

The citizens began to hold gladiator sports clandestinely. Dismayed by the empty seats staring at him, the Emperor decreed that the citizens should come to the amphitheatre whenever an event was held there; if gladiator sports were held secretly, it would be dealt with seriously.

The citizens were now irate; they began to openly revile the Emperor much to the delight of Telemachus.

The baths were an ideal place to spread rumors and indulge in gossip and Telemachus used it to his full advantage.

One day, at the baths, when the Senators were talking in small groups, he deliberately spoke in a raised tone:

'I hear the Emperor is thinking of abolishing slavery.'

The Senators abruptly stopped rambling and turned to Telemachus. Over the past few months he had been gaining their confidence. Even before the formal announcement regarding abolishing gladiator sports had been made, Telemachus had discreetly elicited the information about such a move and had warned the Senators. Hence they were genuinely dismayed when they heard of the latest political reform on the anvil; their aristocratic privileges would crumble if the Emperor were allowed to carry through the same. One by one, the Senators began to speak out their minds

'The Emperor is out of his mind!'

'Have things come to such a pass?'

'He has brought shame to the Empire.'

Then Claudius, a senior and respected Senator spoke out: 'He must be stopped before he does that.'

For a moment there was silence. Then Telemachus seized the opportunity he had been waiting for.

'If I stop him, will you support me?' he asked.

The Senators exchanged meaningful glances. Then all eyes turned to Claudius; it seemed the Senators had unofficially appointed him as their spokesman. At length, Claudius spoke:

'Yes, we will support you. But how do you propose to stop him?'

'I will imprison him today in the night. The citizens will be coming to the arena tomorrow. We will reinstate gladiator sports and explain to them why we overthrew the Emperor. Let them decide his fate,' said Telemachus

All the Senators agreed to Telemachus' plan. The task of explaining to the citizens was entrusted to Claudius, as he was a powerful orator.

The next day, the citizens were waiting impatiently in the amphitheatre, wondering what the Emperor had in store for them. When Claudius was about to make his appearance before the citizens, the Emperor who was now in chains, warned him:

'You will never get away with this. I am aware that my citizens initially disliked me for banning gladiator sports. But never have I acted against my conscience and abolishing gladiator sports was the right thing to do. Any radical reform is likely to meet with resistance initially. But by now good sense must have prevailed over my citizens and they will acquiesce in my reforms. Any right-thinking citizen will never endorse my ouster.'

'Your majesty is so naive. You must feel the pulse of your citizens before you do something. Its not what you think is right that matters, what matters is whether your citizens like it or not. If you want to stay in power, be popular and populist,' Claudius snapped and after a pause added:

'Reforms pushed down the throats of citizens will be purged by them. And, your majesty, citizens are not always right-thinking.'

Then Claudius addressed the citizens:

'Citizens, the past few months we have witnessed one of the most insane decisions ever made by an Emperor in the history of our state. Every citizen has put in his mite in building this great empire and is rightly entitled to have some fun. And what does our Emperor do? He deprives us of that right by banning a glorious sport, which has exhilarated generations and forces us to watch some ludicrous exhibitions of art, which only he can understand. And now he proposes to abolish slavery.'

Claudius waited for his words to sink in. The citizens had received his speech in rapt attention. They began to exchange meaningful glances and there were murmurs of protest against abolishing slavery.

'Here is an Emperor who is afraid of waging a war to expand the glory of our empire and is content to remain within the comforting four walls of his palace. He has relegated our state, which was the epitome of power to an object of ridicule. Do we need such an Emperor?' Claudius asked.

There was silence for some time; then the entire amphitheatre reverberated with a deafening 'No!'

The Emperor was stunned; Claudius and Telemachus exchanged smiles.

'Dear citizens, we have always respected your wishes. To save our state from plunging into further insanity, our great general, Telemachus, has imprisoned the Emperor.'

The crowd greeted this with a resounding applause.

'From today, this arena will once again witness the great fights of our valiant gladiators.'

The crowd was absolutely ecstatic and now began to cheer each sentence that Claudius spoke.

'There shall not be any silly display of arts. And we shall

throw the criminals to the lions for the deaths they deserve.'

Claudius paused for a moment and in a tone tinged with scorn announced: 'Behold your Emperor!'

The Emperor in chains was brought before the crowd. The crowd jeered wildly. The Emperor turned white with fear. Claudius and Telemachus once again exchanged smiles.

'What shall we do with your Emperor?' This time it was Telemachus who spoke.

There was absolute silence for a few moments. Then one of the Senators, as had been planned earlier, shouted, to instigate the crowd: 'Throw him to the lions!'

The spectators were now up to their feet and they roared in unison: 'Throw him to the lions! Throw him to the lions!'

So the King of Kings was freed from his shackles and thrown before the King of Beasts.

He was still in a daze when the hungry lion charged towards him. For the lion, it did not matter whether its prey was a criminal or the Emperor himself. And for the crowd, it did not matter whether the Emperor himself was thrown to the lion, so long as it provided them entertainment.

Once again blood spilled in the amphitheatre.

THE SPORT – A Discussion

'So, what do you think of the Emperor, Anne?' asked Sterling.

'If I were to interpret the parable in business terms,' Anne said, ' I think the Emperor committed the cardinal sin of 'not listening to his customers'; he brought in an 'innovation' that just didn't 'connect with a customer need'. The Emperor did not know his citizens intimately; he also did not realize how his citizens would measure his success. Today you need to be 'market driven'. So listen to people constantly – don't assume that they will like whatever you do. Use customers as your consultants – they know their requirements better than any consultant. Have your finger on the pulse of the customer and deliver what the people want – the right products at the right time. Delivering something 'assuming that people need it' could prove to be a fatal mistake.'

'Anne, I beg to differ on that.' Richard said. 'Today you need to drive markets rather than being driven by markets. I think the Emperor failed because he was a poor communicator; he failed to educate and communicate with his 'customers' and win their confidence. That's why he perished. Let me read out what

Akio Morita says in 'Made In Japan' – 'Our plan is to lead the public with new products rather than ask them what kind of products they want. The public does not know what is possible, but we do. So instead of doing a lot of market research, we refine our thinking on a product and its use and try to create a market for it by educating and communicating with the public.'

'What do you think, Sterling?' Anne asked.

Sterling smiled and said, 'What I intended to convey through this parable was why transformation efforts fail or face such a stiff resistance initially but you have made interesting observations about the role of customers in innovation. Can customers be used as consultants in the innovation process? Well, yes and no. Let me share with you the recent experience of one of my clients which is a gaming company. When this company developed a new game, its customers went to the extent of developing new content for existing games and posting it free on fan web sites. So here is a customer who not only knows what he wants, but also can make what he wants; such a customer is technically competent i.e. he's capable of making changes in the very design of the product; is demanding and actively participates in the creation of value. Also, customer input is valuable in the removing any functional inconvenience or adding any functional convenience to the product. But when you're dealing with a customer who cannot articulate his need, you need to rely on observation and intuition.'

'Has any company adopted this partnership with customer model for innovation?' asked Anne.

'Oh, yes! BMW is one such company. BMW has a Virtual Innovation Agency where anyone can submit an idea for an innovation. In fact a toolkit is posted on its website which lets customers develop ideas showing how the company can make improvements, say in online car services. In fact, BMW was recently awarded the most innovative company in Germany.' said Sterling

'Now let us come back to the discussion on why they empower failed. I think the Emperor failed because in his naivety, he did not take the people affected by the change, into confidence. So the change made no sense to the people. He made no effort to clearly articulate why the change was needed, to search for third alternatives, to establish trust and to develop a shared vision. And that is why, the transformation efforts fail and the bureaucrats take over and status quo prevails. In fact the emperor reminds me of a Chairman who spent 40 billion dollars for new equipment and technological know how .The money vanished into a black hole and the company's market share sank. Why? Because he failed to change the bureaucratic mindset of his organization and take his people into confidence.'

'Also any radical idea is initially politically infeasible. I think any leader who wishes to initiate a reform is faced with the perennial dilemma of choosing between populism and pragmatism' Sterling said. 'As Nobel Laureate Amartya Sen points out, there are three parameters to test the efficacy of economic reforms:

1. Reach: the reach should be such that they should be person-related and the reformers should see what they have done to the lives of the people involved in

the process. The reforms should be evenhanded and all sections should benefit from them, most of all at the bottom of the heap.

2. Range: they should adequately address a broad range of needs.

3. Reason: Reforms need greater reasoning than mere slogans. You must explicitly communicate what you are doing and why you are doing.'

2 | The Temple

General Octavius wondered why the Emperor had summoned him.

'This day the next year marks my twenty-fifth year of reign of the empire. To commemorate this great occasion, I want to build a temple that will be worthy of being called a wonder of the world. I want you to take charge of the construction of the temple. It should be ready for worship before this day, the next year,' the Emperor spoke with gravity.

The General was lost in thought for some time; he was considering how to reply in the most diplomatic manner. He had served the Emperor faithfully for many years and had known him to be arrogant, whimsical and impulsive and he ruled with an iron hand.

At length, the General said, 'Your majesty, I can get a temple built within a year or three months or even three days. But I presume that your majesty's vision is to build a temple that will be admired by posterity as a wonder of the world. For this it must brave the ravages of time like the temple your noble ancestors built. For centuries the temple has remained intact and to this day it stands proudly as a marvel of architecture. But it took three decades and another three days to build the temple.'

'What are you insinuating?' the Emperor asked impatiently.

'That we should focus our energies on building a temple that will last for an eternity rather than building a temple within a year. In other words, it will be impossible to build a temple as envisioned by you within a year; I would humbly request for more time,' the General said as entreatingly as he could but he had committed the cardinal verbal sin of uttering the word 'impossible' – that was the last word the Emperor wanted to hear.

'There is no meaning if the temple cannot be built in a year since the twenty-fifth year of my reign falls next year,' the Emperor said adamantly.

Then you should have had the foresight to plan the construction well in advance, thought the General; he would not normally dare to entertain even a defiant thought before the Emperor.

The Emperor studied the General's face with his piercing eyes as if he was reading his thoughts.

General Octavius was the most trusted and successful General he had; the General had won great wars and built splendid monuments for him. If there was anyone who could build the temple within a year, it was General Octavius.

With a sly smile on his lips and a mischievous twinkle in

his eyes, the Emperor said, 'I take it that you are not confident of taking up the task. I think I will entrust the task to your friend, Protheus. Anyone who completes this task on time will be appointed as the Governor of Ethen.'

Protheus was a powerful general who Octavius considered his toughest competitor in his race for glory and fame and the Emperor was aware of this. Ethen was the most prosperous state in the empire and to be appointed as its Governor was a great honour.

'Your majesty has misunderstood me. It will be a great honour to be entrusted with such a noble task and I am confident of completing it within a year,' Octavius said eagerly.

The Emperor afforded himself a more relaxed smile as the General had taken the bait.

'If you succeed, you can hold your head high and be the Governor of Ethen. But let me warn you, should you fail, you will have no head on your shoulders; I won't stand the slightest failure,' the Emperor said sharply.

The image of his head being severed flashed through the General's mind and he shuddered a little. He knew the Emperor was cold and passionless and would have no qualms in decapitating him, if he failed.

'I understand your majesty,' he said and after bowing before the Emperor, he left.

Building a temple of such size and grandeur required a lot of resources – money, materials and above all slaves.

Hence hundreds of thousands of slaves from every conceivable part of the world were brought to build the great temple. The site of construction became a Babel of cries, moans and sighs in countless dialects but they all spoke of the universal language of human suffering. Soldiers closely supervised these slaves or flogged them as hard as they could and centurions breathed down the necks of soldiers. They knew that if the temple was not built on time, their heads would roll before the General lost his.

Six months passed by and General Octavius had every reason to worry and it was not the physical progress he was actually perturbed with. Barbarians had attacked the empire and its finances were severely under strain. Octavius would have loved to lead the army to war but the responsibility was given to Protheus, as the Emperor wanted the work of the temple to go on unhindered, even in the midst of the bloody war. If Protheus emerged victorious, he would overshadow Octavius and the only way he could mitigate that was to complete the temple within the time and with the reduced inflow of money.

Octavius began to look for ways and means to curtail the cost. It was evident that most of the money was being spent on the slaves. If he could reduce their numbers to half and extract the same amount of work, he could successfully complete his task. There simply had to be fewer mouths to feed!

So began the process of identifying the expendable and the valuable slaves – the weaker and the older ones were deemed to be expendable and the stronger ones were considered valuable – valuable at least till the task was completed. The expendable ones were sold off and if there were no takers, they were beheaded.

It hardly made any difference to the remaining salves whether dawn broke or whether the sun was a blazing sphere or whether it turned crimson or whether the moon and the stars appeared, as they were made to work at a frenzied pace without rest or sleep.

Finally the great temple was built, one month ahead of the schedule.

General Octavius was made the Governor of Ethen.

The day of the consecration of the temple arrived. The Emperor, the High Priest, General Octavius and all the people thronged the temple – all the people, except the slaves who were now languishing in chains, now that the task was completed.

The people stared at this marvel of architecture; they had never seen anything so tall, splendid and colossal. The old temple seemed to pale into insignificance and was now fit only for demolition.

The High Priest began to chant prayers that only he understood. The Emperor who was in a solemn state of piety was suddenly annoyed by something falling on his head; he brushed it aside – it was gravel. He looked at the General; he was also brushing aside gravel. Then more specks of gravel began to fall rapidly. They all looked up with raised eyebrows.

The walls of the temple trembled and the two main pillars of the temple began to give way. At first, their feet were rooted to the ground in mortal fear and then there was a desperate stampede.

The temple that had been built with dangerous haste was now falling apart in a frenzied hurry. In a few moments, the entire temple caved in, killing all the people inside.

All the people, except the salves who were languishing in chains, were killed. With no masters to flog and rule them, they broke off their shackles and became free men.

THE TEMPLE – A Discussion

'The Emperor reminds me of those shareholders and boards that clamor impatiently for instant return on investments and the general, of the CEO who has little time to prove himself. The general had the right vision – building a temple that will last for an eternity rather building it within a year. A temple that is built with dangerous haste will collapse in a frenzied hurry. For everything there should be a foundation. Take the case of customer service. Customer trust is the building block for brand equity, customer ecstasy and repeat business. But often corporations play on imagery to win customers over and then fail to deliver on brand promises. We have seen automobile majors recalling their vehicles and pharmaceutical companies withdrawing drugs, thus creating a crisis of confidence. Only when customer trust is lost, a scramble is made to regain faith and enforce accountability.'

'I think the root cause for all this is because we live in a culture that craves for 'instant gratification'; a culture that thrives on quick fixes which just bring in short term results but create more problems than they solve. What we really need are solid solutions and solid solutions require time, foresight and patience.' Sterling opined.

'Doesn't the parable also reflects how corporations treat their most valuable resources – their people?' Anne said. 'In a good year we bring people in and in a bad year, we fire people and cut back. So how do you expect loyalty from people? I would say the rosy projections that corporations make are to blame for this. The result is over capacity, and then there is a cost cutting spree, the first causality being people. Sterling, even when we go for solid solutions we don't factor people adequately.'

'But how can a company accurately forecast demand? And besides, cut backs are a reality during hard times.' Richard argued.

'Not when company leaders are helping themselves to a hefty bonus!' Anne replied, 'Why can't a substantial part of every employee's total compensation be dependent on company prosperity? That will give everyone incentive to be productive. As regards making unrealistic projections, I feel we are always in the habit of making over optimistic projections. We are so optimistic of success that we do not even entertain pessimistic scenarios. We overestimate the amount of control over the future and also fail to reckon competition. The herd mentality which prompts all companies to follow 'Me-too' strategies is also to blame. How long can the going be so good?' Anne asked.

'You are right, Anne!' Richard said. 'In downturns, one must find ways to work more efficiently. A company cannot afford to look at talent from a cyclical point of view. If it does so, it will end up in not training or investing in people and this will affect business continuity. If money is all we give to employees, we might end up creating a band of mercenaries.'

'Today speed is the key,' Sterling said. 'But in reality speed is often replaced by rashness. That is why the temple that was built with dangerous haste collapsed in a frenzied hurry. The financial scandals that have rocked the corporate world recently show that if values which form the core, the foundation, the very soul of the organization are thrown to the wind, then it can bring even the largest corporations which might have taken decades to build, to its knees within no time. Even in the most turbulent times an organization must never forget its values which extol 'who we are and what we stand for'. You must always take time to build your values and then align resources to those values and strategy before you race to do anything else. A classic case is how Southwest Airlines chose to grow; it chose to grow conservatively, expanding only into one or two cities each year, so that it could devote the necessary time and attention to spread its unique culture in each new city. This brought about a relationship of shared goals, shared knowledge and mutual respect among the employees which has been behind its success even in difficult times. Sustainability and values are inextricably linked. I can only agree with what Henry David Thoreau said:

'If you have built castles in the air, your work need not be lost; that is where they should be. Now put the foundations under them'.

3 | Almarado's Horse

The Captain looked at the peasants who had been lined up to face the firing squad. His eyes were filled with contempt – that was the only emotion he felt for the peasants. But the malicious smile that always lingered on his lips was absent; instead the features of his face had turned wry with worry.

The firing squad was waiting for the Captain's order to fire. But the Captain was looking around impatiently – apparently he was expecting someone. He was desperately hoping that Almarado would turn up and he could turn up any instant and vanish the next moment, once again eluding the clutches of law.

It was a time when the feudal lords ruled indiscriminately. Only one man dared to take up arms against the unjust system and that man was Almarado. Hence he was the darling of the masses and a thorn in the flesh for the Captain who had promised the lords to capture the bandit at any cost. But all his attempts to apprehend him had been futile.

There were no charges against the peasants who were facing the firing squad; they were merely pawns in the sinister ploy employed by the Captain to draw out Alamarado from his lair and trap him.

But still there was no sign of Alamarado.

Finally, the Captain gave the order to fire.

But just when the soldiers were about to fire, there was a whipping sound and before they could realize what was happening, their rifles were thrown out of their hands.

'Alamarado!' shouted the peasants with joy and hope.

'Almarado!' the Captain said in a tone that was barely a whisper.

Almarado, as usual, had appeared in the nick of time. With one slick manoeuvre of the whip, he had wrapped all the rifles and tugged at them, disarming the firing squad instantly.

'Catch him!' yelled the Captain, when he got back his breath.

The soldiers drew their swords and surrounded Almarado. But Almarado was the most skilled swordsman in the land and soon all the soldiers found themselves lying on the ground, either wounded or disarmed and certainly helpless.

'Catch him! Catch him!' the Captain shouted in dismay; he was behaving like a child who throws up tantrums when his favourite candy is snatched away from him.

A grinning Almarado next freed the peasants and then whistled. Hearing the familiar whistle, a black stallion galloped towards Almarado. It was Black Storm, Almarado's horse.

'Stop him! Stop him!' screamed the Captain; he knew that once Almarado mounted the horse, it would be impossible to catch him, for Black Storm was the fastest and the smartest stallion in the land. But no one could prevent Almarado from mounting Black Storm and speeding away. The soldiers mounted their horses and chased him. The captain felt like tearing his hair away.

Almarado shot a quick glance over his shoulder. The soldiers were following in hot pursuit. Then he looked ahead and was relieved to find that he was nearing a chasm that was deep and wide. He smiled.

'Jump! Black Storm, jump!' he shouted.

Black Storm surged; he cleared the yawning chasm in one effortless leap and disappeared into the woods on the other side with his master, who could not help laughing as he imagined the plight of the soldiers.

The horses of the soldiers stopped abruptly in their tracks as they reached the chasm and refused to jump. The soldiers cursed their horses and their luck once again and returned, empty-handed.

In the past few months, whenever they gave Almarado the chase, it invariably culminated in this clichéd ending. The chasm and Black Storm always stood in their way. They wished they had a stallion like Black Storm.

Black Storm was perhaps the greatest gift that Almarado received from his father. His father, after whom he had been named, was himself a outlaw who was the champion of the downtrodden in his heyday. As he grew old he was wise enough to realize that he could not continue his good work forever. Hence he had meticulously trained Almarado Junior to take off from where he left. He made him a skilled swordsman with lightning reflexes and an adroit rider.

Black Storm served his young master as faithfully as he had served his old master. He was Almarado Senior's second horse; he had ridden him during the last years of his life as a bandit.

One day as the Junior Almarado emerged out of his hideout to ride Black Storm to another adventure, he found his father stroking the horse fondly and at the same time regarding it thoughtfully.

'Don't you think it's time that you replaced Black Storm?' he asked suddenly.

The question caught the junior unawares. He reflected for a while; during the past few months Black Storm had slowed down a little and the gap between him and the horses of the soldiers had slightly narrowed but it was still comfortable and he still managed to clear the chasm with relative ease.

'No, I think he still has a few more years in him. Besides I am very comfortable with him. If I get a new horse I will have to train him and he might make mistakes. And besides where do I have the time? Good old Black Storm!'

Almarado Junior patted his horse proudly.

'When age stands in the way of discharge of duty, then you must retire before you become a liability; that's why I retired. Otherwise I would have been languishing in prison by now. Now its time for Black Storm to retire. So I think you must find time to look for a new horse.' Almarado Senior said sharply.

'I will think over it,' Almarado Junior said as he mounted Black Storm.

'Remember Black Storm is not getting any younger and the chasm is not getting any narrower,' the old man warned.

But his son only smiled and he rode away. The old man shook his head.

It was another daring caper and when Almarado mounted Black Storm, he knew he had almost pulled it off. Now everything depended on Black Storm.

Almarado suddenly felt that Black Storm was not in his elements that day. As he glanced over his shoulder, he was shocked to see the soldiers closing in.

'Go! Black Storm, go!' he egged Black Storm.

The soldiers started firing. Almarado suddenly felt an incisive pain in his right shoulder; blood was gushing from his right shoulder; he was hit! Panic seized him.

There had been many narrow escapes but never had he been wounded in his encounters.

As he neared the chasm, the routine optimism he always experienced gave way to growing trepidation.

Will Black Storm clear the chasm? He wondered.

As the soldiers saw Black Storm approaching the edge of the chasm, they almost gave up hope.

Black Storm leaped, his eyes clearly fixed on the other side of the chasm. And he almost cleared the chasm. But when a chasm so wide and deep had to be cleared, the difference between clearing it completely and almost clearing it meant the difference between life and death.

And Black Storm had only *almost* cleared it.

For a moment, Almarado was petrified. He was thrown off his saddle. A cry of horror welled up from his parched throat as he realized that he and Black Storm were plunging into the jaws of death. His head seemed to throb with the words of advice of his father.

Black Storm was the first to touch the bottom of the chasm, followed by Almarado. They lay at the bottom of the chasm in a pool of blood, never to ride again together.

ALMARADO'S HORSE – A Discussion

'The parable reminds me of the need to manage the life cycle of brands' Richard said. 'Brands that do not change with the times, will grow old and inevitably die and will drag the company along with them to certain death just like Almarado and his horse. Even mature brands need to 'build in change' in their model as nothing stays the same in the same way. Successful brands retain their core values while constantly reinventing brand intangibles to remain relevant to consumer needs. I feel that franchises like James Bond, Star Wars, Harry Porter etc. have remained successful because their creators realized this. Otherwise your market share will be slowly eaten into by rival brands and you will be caught napping and you will disappear from the mind space of the consumer.'

'You are absolutely right, Richard!' Anne exclaimed, 'Our Company just went through a similar learning experience. We had a venerable brand which was our major brand and we were facing sluggish sales. It was then we realized that we could no longer sell what we produced but had to produce what we could sell. We had a target audience that grew up with more exiting options than our traditional brand. They just didn't grow up with this brand or rather we hadn't grown up with them because lifestyle and excitement was simply missing in our brand. It is then you realize that there is this 'chasm' or gulf that you have to bridge between the customer expectations and our deliverables. Today we have realigned our business to a diversified customer profile.'

'The parable is reflective of often what happens to 'heritage brands' – brands which have built a loyal customer base over the years. Often such brands commit the fatal mistake of being true to their heritage instead of the customer. Quality and reliability that brought you heritage is not sufficient to survive; it can at best guarantee nostalgia; you also need differentiation and relevance – the brand intangibles you were referring to, Richard. You need to tell an engaging story to stay connected to your customer. One such brand that initially floundered by focusing too much on heritage was Mac Donald. But they soon got their act together by first expanding their offering to include salads among other things. And today, salads from an integral part of the health conscious customer's quick meals. The second thing they did was to re-connect with those people who had made them so popular in the first place – people who were kids a decade or two ago through their new ad campaign 'I'm lovin' it!'. Sometimes you need to kill a brand to keep the customer and you can see that Almarado is hesitant to let Black Storm go because of nostalgia. So you need to continually check whether your 'horse' – your ideas, processes, products, brands or methods – 'is getting old'. Otherwise you will not clear the 'chasm.' Sterling said.

4 Damsels in Distress

The Queen was fighting for her life; she had been poisoned. The physician after examining her spoke solemnly to the worried King.

'Only one herb can save the Queen and that can be found only in the mount of Mesuvis. The mount is far far away and if you ride on your fastest horse you may be able to return just before night. Hence you must send your most dependable man to fetch this herb and bring it to me before night falls, so that I can make the antidote and save the Queen. Till such time, my medicines can only delay death.'

The King had no doubts as to who he should send on a mission of such grave importance and urgency; it had to be Sir Lancelot. He was the bravest, best and the worthiest knight in the kingdom and certainly the most trusted and dependable.

So the King summoned Sir Lancelot and entrusted him with the task.

The physician described to the knight how the herb would look like and where to find it in the mount.

'Remember, should you fail to bring the herb before night falls, the poison will take its toll and we will not be able to save the Queen,' the physician warned him.

Sir Lancelot began to polish his armour. It was going to be a long and arduous journey and he wanted the beautiful maidens he might see on the way, to take notice of him, as he gallantly galloped past them, with their hearts fluttering with the question:

'Who is this dashing, handsome knight in shining armour?'

He polished his armour till he could see his reflection on it. While he stood admiring his armour, the King walked in.

'Sir Lancelot, haven't you started yet?' he asked impatiently.

'I am leaving, your majesty. You can put aside your fears and count on me to fetch the herb on time,' said Sir Lancelot pompously. Then he armed himself with his sword, lance and shield, put on his shining armour, mounted his white stallion and sped away.

He had covered a quarter of the distance, when he heard a lady crying out for help. He reined in his horse and listened to the voice – it was beautiful and going by the voice, the damsel in distress was also likely to be beautiful.

Sir Lancelot's mind was assailed by many questions. Should he help this damsel in distress? But if he took a detour, wouldn't it delay the mission for which he had set out? But at the same time, how could he ignore the appeal of a lady direly in need of help; wasn't it against chivalry? He felt he had enough time to help this dame.

Hence Sir Lancelot turned his horse in the direction from which he heard the cry for help. It was a beautiful princess and a dragon had attacked her castle. Sir Lancelot drew his sword from his sheath and charged towards the dragon, challenging it. A fierce fight ensued and in the end he slew the dragon but the dragon had burnt his right arm.

The townsfolk gave him a rousing welcome. As the princess nursed his right hand, she looked at him with admiring eyes; evidently she had fallen in love with this daring knight. In the midst of the celebration, Sir Lancelot suddenly remembered that he had a mission to accomplish. He promised the townsfolk and the princess that he would return one day.

When it was time to leave, Sir Lancelot asked the princess, 'Will you honour me by giving me a favour?'

The princess was overjoyed and she gave him her favourite red scarf. She then bade him goodbye with tears in her eyes. Sir Lancelot mounted his faithful stallion and egged it, to make up for the lost time.

He had covered more than half the distance, when he heard a lady's cry of despair; it was an old lady. Once again his mind raced with disturbing questions. Chivalry demanded that he should help the lady but his sense of priority urged him to reach the mount at least before dusk. But he had covered more than half the distance and he could trust his stallion to make up for the lost time. There was no harm in at least finding out what disturbed the lady. Once again he took a detour.

The old lady was greatly relieved to see the gallant knight; Sir Lancelot's majestic presence itself was enough to instill hope and confidence in any heart filled with dismay.

'O valiant knight! Some notorious outlaws have abducted my daughter. The leader of the outlaws wants to forcibly marry her. I beg you to kindly rescue her,' she pleaded.

Sir Lancelot looked at the old lady with pity; in her prime she must have been a lovely dame and so her daughter was likely to be comely. It was 'unknightly' to ignore her.

'I will certainly rescue your daughter; have no fear,' Sir Lancelot assured her.

The old lady showed the knight the direction that the bandits had taken and the great knight wended his way through. It led him to the woods where the outlaws had retired. He spotted them and the young maiden who had been abducted – she was breathtakingly beautiful!

Sir Lancelot discreetly hid the favour he had received from the princess.

'Release the fair maiden or die!' Sir Lancelot warned the bandits as he brandished his sword at them.

The bandits only laughed it away; there were ten of them and they thought the foolhardy knight stood no chance of even defending himself. They decided to fight the knight for the sake of amusement.

As his right arm had been badly burnt, Sir Lancelot's reflexes were not as swift as he had expected but he was still more than a match for the bandits. When he had either killed or mortally wounded five of the bandits, the rest of the bandits realized that they had grossly underestimated their adversary and took to their heels. Sir Lancelot wiped the sweat from his forehead and looked at the maiden and his eyes met her admiring gaze. Suddenly, he felt a gnawing pain in his left arm; one of the bandits had plunged his dagger deep into his left arm and blood streamed from the wound. He pulled the dagger and hurled it away and winced as he did so.

The lady woke up from her trance and exclaimed, 'O dashing knight! I can never thank you enough for saving me. Oh! Your left arm is bleeding!'

The lady took Sir Lancelot to a lake nearby and washed his wounds with tender care. Sir Lancelot was wondering which of the ladies he had rescued was the more beautiful one – certainly the second one was more beautiful; but the first one was a princess. The maiden applied some herbs she found in the woods to the wound. This reminded Sir Lancelot of the herb in search of which he had set out.

'Fair maiden, I must take leave of you now. I have been sent by my King on an important mission and I must reach Mount Mesuvis before dusk,' said Sir Lancelot.

'But sire, Mount Mesuvis is miles away and you will not

be able to reach there before dusk however furiously you ride. Besides you are badly wounded and are in no condition to travel!' the maiden wailed, her voice full of concern.

'I can't wait for my wounds to heal but do not worry lady, for my stallion will take me there at the speed of wind,' Sir Lancelot said.

The incurably romantic knight then made a request that the maiden just could not turn down. Her heart brimming with love for the gallant knight, she gave him her favourite white scarf. Then she bade him goodbye, with tears in her eyes.

Sir Lancelot looked at the sky; in a few hours it would be dusk. He began to grow anxious. He spurred his stallion forward and then he felt severe pain in both his arms.

The stallion realizing its master's urgency, dashed as fast as it could but by the time they reached Mount Mesuvis, it had grown dark and it was not possible to trace the herb.

Sir Lancelot hung his head in shame; his heart was heavy with remorse. Now there was no hope of saving the Queen. For the first time, he had failed the King. He did not have the temerity to return to the kingdom and show his pennant. So he wandered aimlessly.

He stopped for the night at a hamlet. He did not reveal his name; he introduced himself as a wandering knight in search of adventure. The villagers considered it a great honour to welcome a knight to their hamlet. Sir Lancelot enthralled them by narrating his daring adventures.

After dinner, the head of the hamlet looked meaningfully at the villagers and then turned to the knight. 'Sire, you seem to be a godsend. For long, ghouls have ravaged our hamlet. In the dead of the night, they stalk our people, snatch them away to some unknown land and devour them. We...'

Before he could complete, his lovely daughter, looked imploringly at the knight with her lovely eyes and chirped in, 'O gallant knight! We beseech you – deliver us from these ghouls!'

Sir Lancelot mused for a while; he was weary and weak and was in acute pain but again here was another damsel in distress in need of his help. Once again gallantry and chivalry got the better of him.

'The evil ghouls will not trouble you again. Trust me,' he said, brimming with confidence.

That night, Sir Lancelot and a few villagers armed with scythes and axes kept watch. When it was past midnight, growing trepidation was evident on the faces of the villagers. There was an eerie silence; suddenly the inhuman cries of the ghouls rang in the air. The villagers who had kept watch along with Sir Lancelot were struck with panic and deserted him, leaving him to fend for himself.

Sir Lancelot struck down the ghouls dead, one by one. But it was a most savage fight and his armour could not prevent the ghouls from inflicting mortal wounds with their fangs and claws. As he drove his blade through the last ghoul, he felt life ebbing out of his body; he staggered and collapsed to the ground. When the villagers were sure that the fight had ended, they came out of their homes. They were relieved to find they had been finally rid of their scourge.

But the brave knight had laid down his life.

The villagers buried the knight with the greatest honour they could accord – they laid him to rest in his shining armour, alongwith his sword, lance and shield and a red scarf and a white scarf.

Before Sir Lancelot set off, the King had promised him: 'Sir Lancelot, if you save the Queen's life, I will make you Seneschal of all my lands.'

But now he lay buried, an obscure knight in an obscure hamlet, with these words inscribed on his tombstone:

'Here lies the valiant knight who saved this hamlet from the ghouls.'

DAMSELS IN DISTRESS – A Discussion

'The knight could have become Seneschal but instead takes many detours and finally dies as an obscure knight. We too often resemble the knight. In the twilight of our lives, we look back and feel remorse at what we could have become because we never fully achieve our potential. This can happen to you if you don't 'begin with the end in mind' as Stephen Covey puts it. You need to ask yourself what is the legacy I would like to be behind? How would I like to be remembered even when I am dead and gone?' Anne said.

'I agree with you'. Richard said. 'You need to continually prioritize and focus on the 'big picture' and to pursue it relentlessly, instead of getting distracted by trivial things and get lost in the maze. I have seen companies fail due to an overload of initiatives because of its inability to discern what is important. This creates confusion and dissipates time, energy and money and achieves precious little. Strategy, after all, is about choices and trade-offs. As Micheal Porter points out it is a race to get to the position you want to occupy and in that process, one must be prepared to make trade-offs that is forsake some options. One has to stick to one's core competencies and have real focus'.

'But you must be careful not to let your core competencies become core incompetencies.' Sterling said.

'Core Incompetency? What do you mean by that?' Richard asked.

'Well, I was thinking of this IT company which is content on doing back-end job and picking up the low hanging fruit. It believes that this job is its core competence but if it doesn't go up the value chain, pick the high hanging fruit and learn to create higher value it might become its core incompetence. What will happen if some lower cost company comes in and undercuts? So your competence might become incompetence in a different context.' Sterling said.

'I think Walgreens' case study is very relevant in this context.' Anne said. 'The company decided to exit food service business which was not only the largest part of its business but which was also a long standing family tradition. Why? Because the company realized that it could be the best in the world at convenience drugstores. So the company exited its traditional business in five years and focused all its resources on where its brightest future lay-convenience drug stores. And hasn't Walgreens proved itself right today? What would have happened if it had stuck to its restaurant business believing that it is its core competency?'

'One has to stick to one's core competencies and have real focus but focus on the context; it is the context that determines the relevance of your competence. And focus reminds me of Robert Frost's lines.' Sterling said and he began to recite them:

'The woods are lovely, dark and deep

But I have promises to keep

And miles to go before I sleep

And miles to go before I sleep.'

5 | The Fortress

The Astors were invincible warriors. Since they lead a nomadic life, they completely destroyed the cities they captured and either killed or enslaved the citizens. No one could withstand their onslaught and city after city was annexed to their empire.

Even the gods dreaded them.

Gradually the Astors grew tired of their wandering life. Winning battles had now become a habit for them and had ceased to be challenging. They had a vast empire which included most of the then known world. They now desired to settle down. So they began to build a formidable fortress and a magnificent city within the fortress

The hands that wielded swords now held whips to flog the slaves.

Finally they built an imposing fortress that threatened to pierce the sky and inside the fortress was a gem of a city. It was for the first time that the Astors had constructed such splendid structures. They had now proved that they were equally good at construction as they were at destruction.

As the Astors lay low, their enemies gained in strength. They united and a combined army laid siege to the fortress. But their attempts to breach the fortress were in vain.

No one could scale such heights; no battering ram or siege engine could make any dent on the fortress.

The Astors did not even care to retaliate. From their lofty fortress, they watched with scorn their enemies making abortive attempts. After months of frustration, their enemies finally retreated.

The Astors were delighted; they declared: 'This fortress is impregnable. So let us eat, drink, make merry and never worry.'

They now felt that no one was even required to stand guard

Decades passed by

The enemies of the Astors once again laid siege to the fortress. This time they brought cannons with them. The Astors had resigned themselves to a life of pleasure and were blissfully unaware of the invention of cannons.

It was a silent night and the Astors were fast asleep. Suddenly, the stillness of the night was shattered by the deafening thunder of the cannons.

The Emperor of the Astors was rudely jolted from his

peaceful sleep from what he thought was heavy thunder. He could hear the clash of steel and hoarse cries – the cries of soldiers engaged in a battle. He wondered whether there had been a rebellion.

A soldier barged into his chambers, panting.

'Your majesty! We have been attacked by our enemies...and they have already penetrated the fortress!' he blurted out.

'Impossible! The fortress can never fall!' the Emperor shouted in utter disbelief.

'Your majesty, they have strange weapons with them... barrels on wheels that spit fire and thunder.... they have breached the fortress with these weapons and they are pouring in,' the soldier said, haltingly.

The Emperor regarded the soldier thoughtfully. He could not comprehend fully what the soldier was spouting. He couldn't believe that his enemies had dared to enter his city and now that they had done so, they had to be routed and his sons could easily carry out that task.

'My sons will drive them away like cattle. Do not disturb me,' the Emperor said. He then tried to shut his ears to the earsplitting boom of the cannons and drift away to sleep.

After some time, the Emperor was exasperated at being woken up by the soldier again.

Hadn't he told unequivocally that he was not to be disturbed?

'Your majesty, they have killed all your sons!' the soldier wailed.

It took some time for the Emperor to absorb the shocking news and then his drowsiness vanished in a trice and he was spurred into action.

'Bring me my sword!' he ordered

By the time the soldier turned to fetch the sword, the enemies had forced their way into the room. Their swords were dripping with blood.

'Now you can join your sons!' he heard them contemptuously say as they brought down their swords on him. Those were the last words the Emperor heard in his life.

The Astors had been completely caught unawares. They were seeing cannons for the first time and they were stunned by their destructive power. They scrambled for their weapons; they had even forgotten where they had kept them. Their swords had gathered rust and cobwebs and their minds had forgotten the art of warfare. They had been invincible warriors once but that day they were no match for their enemies and they were all killed or enslaved.

Before they left, the enemies razed the city and the fortress to the ground with cannonade.

THE FORTRESS – A Discussion

'Complacency is the biggest corporate killer,' Anne said. 'Business history is littered with the great falls of the mighty organizations, once considered infallible and they fall ignominiously from former glory. Past success is past.'

'Till the time they built the fortress,' Anne continued, 'the Astors were wandering and winning battles. It's like being on the path of 'sustaining innovation'. Once that stops their fall is inevitable. As Jack Welch points out 'there is no ultimate victory in the new economy; there is only having the strength to battle another day.'

'I would add that the parable also points out the inevitability of strategy decay,' Richard said. 'We live in such a turbulent environment that the greatest challenge that an organization faces is not 'sustaining innovation' but how it is able to anticipate and adapt to 'disruptive innovation' which simply destroys all existing business models. In the case of the Astors, they were blissfully unaware that the battering ram and siege engine had been replaced by cannons and still the Emperor tries to shut his ears to the sound of cannons.'

'But Richard' asked Anne, 'how can 'disruptive

innovation' take place within an existing structure?'

'No, it can't take place within an existing structure,' Richard answered 'That's why you need to continually ignore the existing structures to let new businesses in. I believe that disruptive innovation can take place only outside an existing structure. So you need to take your brightest minds outside the existing structure and let them loose. What do you say, Sterling?'

'I think the research of Michael. L.Tushman, professor of management at Harvard Business School is very relevant.' Sterling said. 'He advocates the creation of an ambidextrous organization where two units are allowed to co-exist, one which focuses on incremental innovation whereas the other focuses on disruptive innovation. They are allowed to have their own unique processes and cultures but there is strong coordination and integration at top management. An example for this is USA today, where three businesses – newspaper, television and the web are allowed to run independently but the heads of these businesses meet everyday to discuss synergies and iron out differences.'

'This parable is about complacency. We often underestimate the complexity of the world around us. We believe that our lives will go on for ever and nothing will stop us in our tracks. So we build walls around us – walls of self-deception and we live and strive in terms of the needs and desires that pertain to us, as if we are in a secure fortress. We don't reach out beyond ourselves. And one day our walls are torn away by disruptive forces that we never expected, like September 11 and SARS. So I think only the paranoid, the proactive and the resilient will survive.' Sterling concluded.

6 | The Bells

There the bells go again! thought the King as he heard the bells ringing for the seventh time during that day and just when he was about to sign perhaps the most important treaty in the history of his kingdom.

He looked helplessly into the eyes of his guest with an apologetic smile on his lips. His guest was no ordinary man – he was the King of a faraway and prosperous land. For the past few days, they had been holding important discussions regarding the possibility of trade between the two countries.

And the bells had continually interrupted the discussions.

He had noticed that his guest was finding it hard to conceal his exasperation. After all, his guest had come all the way from a distant land and wasn't it his duty to give his guest his undivided attention?

Yet each time the bells rang, he had to apologise and go out.

The first king, who ruled over the country, had installed these bells. He had the bells installed as a token of his gratitude to the people who had chosen him to be the king. At any time of the day or night, any subject with any grievance could walk in and ring the bell and the king was bound to resolve the grievance immediately.

At that time the population was thin and the king knew each of his subjects by name. But over the years the kingdom expanded rapidly and the population multiplied manifold. But still the tradition continued and the bells bore testimony to the selfless service rendered by the kings.

The present king found these bells particularly irritating. When he was in the midst of a grave discussion, the bell would ring and he had to terminate the discussion and attend to the grievance. When he was having his meals, the bell would again ring and he would have to rush out. After a hard day's work when he was just drifting to a peaceful sleep, the bell would again ring. But he had to carry out the last advice that his father had given him on his deathbed:

'Remember son, when the bell rings, however important the work you are doing at that time, set it aside and immediately attend to the grievances of your people; for nothing is more important than resolving the grievances of your subjects.'

But he was now finding it impossible to think, eat or even sleep….. peacefully.

When the treaty had been finally signed and the guest seen off, the King called his advisor to his chambers. The advisor had been his tutor from childhood.

'I am thinking of removing those bells,' the King said

The advisor looked at him as if he had committed the most deplorable sin he could think of.

'How can you ever think of that? That would be dereliction of duty; you are a servant of your people and the problems of your people are your first priority,' he protested.

'Revered Sir, I only intend to serve my kingdom better by removing those bells'

'And pray, how would that be possible?'

'Just think of all the grievances that I attend everyday. Most of them are trivial; even silly. Do you need a king to attend to such matters? Why! An ordinary man with common sense can solve these problems. A king's time is precious and there are larger and graver issues to attend to.'

'So what are you suggesting?'

'Divide the kingdom into ten provinces. Identify eleven men; men with common sense; men who are practical. Sir, I would like you to identify these men and teach them the laws of our land just as you have taught me. Make eleven copies of our books of law to which only you and I had access hitherto and give to them. When their training is complete, the wisest among them will be appointed at the palace as the chief counselor and the rest will be placed in charge of the provinces. Let the people approach them.

At the beginning of every week let them assemble in the palace, under the guidance of the chief counselor and discuss among themselves any issues that they have not been able to resolve. If they still are not able to arrive at some solutions, let the chief counselor discuss with you and me. In other words, I will only be dealing with those problems of my people that the council is not able to solve. That will leave me sufficient time to deal with other important issues,' the King said.

The advisor's eyes lit up

'Why didn't someone think of this before? But what if they make mistake?' the advisor asked.

'Ah! We should be able to live with that, for the time being. They should be allowed to make mistakes but they should not make the same mistake twice,' the King said

The search for the eleven wisest men began. Meanwhile eleven copies of the books of law were made. The eleven men were identified and taken to the palace. There the advisor taught them the laws of the land just as he had taught the King. Whenever the bells rang, the King took the eleven men with him so that they could get a first hand knowledge of how he dealt with the problems of his people. Gradually they began to solve the problems of the people in the presence of the King.

The King then divided the kingdom into ten provinces. The wisest among them was appointed at the palace as the chief counselor and the remaining ten men were placed in charge of the ten provinces. The King then gave orders that the decisions of the ten men would be binding on the people. But he also made it clear in the order that he did not mean to distance himself from his dear subjects and he only wanted to serve them better.

At first the people were unhappy since the direct access to the King that they had enjoyed was now denied. They reluctantly approached the ten men. Soon they realized that the ten men were solving their problems just as their King would solve them; besides they didn't have to travel all the way to the palace.

At the beginning of every week the ten men assembled in the palace, under the guidance of the chief counselor and discussed among themselves issues that they were not able to resolve. If they still were not able to arrive at solutions, the chief counselor discussed the same with the King and the advisor.

The King could now focus on important issues.

The bells were removed from the palace.

The King could now think, eat and sleep... peacefully.

THE BELLS – A Discussion

'I think the parable is a classic case of Empowerment,' Anne said. 'First, the King shares information with the counselors; mistakes are allowed to be made and viewed as learning opportunities. Next he creates autonomy by clarifying roles, training them, giving them resources and making them accountable for results. Finally he replaces the old hierarchy with the empowered counselors. A new model leader is not a corporate dictator. Unfortunately, many leaders feel that it is good to have control and they become addicted to power – and that is what kills companies. This is the age of empowerment and the ability to effectively delegate is critically important for its success. The purpose of leadership is to create leaders at all levels and empowerment is the key to that.'

'One of my favorites is Ricardo Semler,' Sterling said. 'I think his leadership at SEMCO is revolutionary – he has taken work place democracy to previously unimagined frontiers. Everyone at the company has access to the books; managers set their own salaries; shop floor workers set their own productivity targets and schedules; workers make decisions that were once the preserve of managers.'

'But isn't this all Utopian?' Richard asked

' Richard, the results speak for themselves.' Sterling said. 'SEMCO has managed to buck the Brazilian commercial chaos, hyperinflation of almost 900 % and recession to increase productivity nearly sevenfold and profits five fold. It is said that during negotiations over a new labor contract, a union leader argued that too big a raise would over extend the company.'

'Now that's interesting!' Richard said, ' I would also like to add that, the king was successful because he applied the 80/20 rule – that is concentrating on those critical activities which really give him a return on his time. It's a great human tragedy that we spend proportionately too much time on small decisions and not enough on the really big ones'

'Have you guys noted one thing?' Sterling asked, 'That we often delegate or fail to delegate for the wrong reasons. We hold on to tasks which we like to do – not which make the best use of our time and delegate 'distasteful' tasks.''

'A lot of considerations are to be weighed before deciding what should and should not be delegated.' echoed Richard. 'For example however big my company might grow, Mark & Co, my first major client will always get my personal attention. I am not going to delegate that to anyone.'

'So you should delegate what you can, not what you want to.' Anne concluded.

7 | The Dragon Slayer

A fiery dragon ravaged the land of Naomi. It would appear all of a sudden, breathing fire, and set ablaze houses and fields and kill the hapless people. Then it would disappear as suddenly as it had appeared, leaving behind a trial of death and destruction. The Queen of Naomi had gone to visit the neighbouring kingdom and hence the Council of Ministers urgently sought the services of Sir Grimlet, the Dragon Slayer.

Sir Grimlet dashed to Naomi. He had slain many dragons and was anxious to slay more and earn more fame and money. The people of Naomi were impressed and convinced by his very appearance – his shining armour, his white magnificent horse and an array of weapons that seemed deadly. For six days there was no sign of the dragon; the people of Naomi thought that the dragon had fled for its life sensing Sir Grimlet's arrival.

But on the seventh day the dragon appeared, wreaking havoc and destruction.

Sir Grimlet rushed to the scene of destruction. It was the biggest and the most ferocious dragon Sir Grimlet had encountered but that did not unsettle him in any way. Sir

Grimlet used one weapon after the other in his arsenal. Blood gushed from the dragon's wounds but its fury continued unabated. With a twist of its tail, it knocked down Sir Grimlet from his horse. The onlookers missed a heartbeat. But Sir Grimlet was quickly on his feet and as the dragon swooped down to attack him, he delved his spear deep into the dragon's heart. The dragon winced, let out a shattering cry of pain and dropped to the ground with a resounding thud. It lay there writhing, as if desperately trying to ward off imminent death but after a few moments it became completely still.

When the people got their breath restored, they broke into uproarious cheers.

'Sire, we can never thank you enough for saving us from this dragon! When the Queen returns tomorrow she will honour you in her court,' the Council of Ministers told Sir Grimlet as he wiped drops of blood and sweat from his face.

The next day, it was a packed gathering at the Queen's court. Sir Grimlet was the cynosure of all eyes and he held himself gallantly erect. They were all waiting for the Queen to speak who strangely seemed to be in a pensive mood.

'Why did you kill the dragon?' the Queen asked gravely.

There was a stunned silence and Sir Grimlet was completely taken aback.

'Why did I kill the dragon? Why! Your Council of Ministers sought my services and I slew the dragon,' Sir

Grimlet explained.

'The Council of Ministers has no authority to make such requests; not when the Queen is still alive,' snapped the Queen.

One of the ministers rose to explain.

'Your majesty, you were away and we had to act immediately. The dragon...'

The Queen raised her hand and the Minister stopped abruptly as if an invisible hand had clutched his throat. He sat down with a sullen expression on his face.

'Sir Grimlet, I demand to know why you slew the poor dragon,' the Queen asked with gravity.

'Then what am I supposed to do? Fall in love with the dragon? I am a professional dragon slayer; I slay dragons.... that's my job,' Sir Grimlet said; he was now getting impatient.

'Do you know it is against the law of our land to kill animals?' the Queen asked

'I don't think the dragon can be considered as an animal,' replied Sir Grimlet

'Well, I consider it as an animal... a rare, colourful, vibrant animal that breathes fire and that's what matters. You should have captured it alive and we could have tamed it. Look at this once ferocious tiger that is lying at my feet like a cute cat.... I tamed it personally. Ah! Only if you hadn't slain that poor dragon! Whenever we wanted fire we could have trained it to spit fire and we could fly on it to wherever we wanted to.... there are scores of things we could have done. And I would have been the proud mistress of the first pet dragon in the world. I simply adore these four-legged creatures and I will do everything in my power to protect them. After all, they are better than the two-legged variety around me,' said the Queen, as she looked contemptuously at the Council of Ministers.

Sir Grimlet was clearly exasperated.

'Will I be rewarded for my services?' he asked.

'Reward you for your services!' the Queen sneered. 'According to the law of our land, anyone who kills an animal will be imprisoned and the Queen will decide the terms of imprisonment based on the severity of the crime.'

Sir Grimlet decided to be diplomatic for the last time.

'Your majesty, with all due respect to you, were you expecting me to wade through all the law books of the land when the savage dragon was on the rampage? I had to act swiftly to put an end to the carnage. And the law should after all be interpreted pragmatically.'

'How dare you give me unsolicited advice, you...you heartless dragon slayer? Soldiers! Arrest this insolent man immediately!' screamed the Queen.

This time Sir Grimlet decided to let his sword 'do the

talking'. He over powered the soldiers, mounted his horse and sped away, leaving everyone in the court spellbound at the pace at which he had deftly managed his escape.

Sir Grimlet's next halt was the land of Saomi, which had also been troubled by a dragon. When he reached there, the dragon was going berserk and the soldiers were desperately trying to ward it off. The King was relieved to see Sir Grimlet. But Sir Grimlet seemed to be in no hurry to slay the dragon; instead he calmly rode to the King.

'I want to pore over all your law books to see if there is any law which will hinder my work or render it invalid. If there are no such laws, I want you to sign this contract which expressly spells out the terms and conditions of my engagement and which absolves me of any liability. And I want half of my reward in advance.' Sir Grimlet said with all graveness he could muster.

'But Sire.... the dragon!' the baffled King protested.

'Let the whole of Saomi be burnt in the dragon's fire.... I don't care. But first where are the rules?'

THE DRAGON SLAYER – A Discussion

'Dogmatism and Bureaucracy are the biggest killers of ideas and action.' Anne observed 'It breeds procrastination and paralysis by analysis, instead of appreciating any completed action by people. One cannot let policies stifle operation.'

'I fully agree with you, Anne.' Richard said, 'Business is about action – a bias for action is what often separates a successful company from an also-ran. Hence it cannot afford to get wedded to polices and procedures which are not relevant. I have often encountered companies with ridiculously restrictive policies that prevented them from seizing a major business opportunity. In every company you come across 'procedurcrats' like the Queen who don't care *what* is being done but *how* it is being done and stifle initiative and dampen enthusiasm in the process. That is why someone said that you need to have an expiry date even for policies.'

'True, such absurd rules pop up every now and then; sometimes they are so absurd you wonder how anyone thought them up.' Sterling said. 'One should not create a culture that rewards mindless conformity and leaves behind anachronisms. And SEMCO is one company that passionately believes this. A new employee joining

SEMCO gets today a 28 page booklet called the 'Survival Manual' which has a lot of cartoons but few words. This is the only written set of rules. The basic message-use your common sense.'

'Rules are virtue but not the only virtue. People are more important. And sometimes to succeed, you need to break all rules in the rulebook.' Sterling concluded.

8 | Once I was a Prince

The beggar sat on the pavement, looking around with an empty sort of avidity. Whenever the passersby dropped alms, he would give a self-deprecating laugh and mutter:

'Once I was a Prince.'

It was true. He had been the Crown Prince once. And then, he had fallen madly in love with a beautiful peasant girl and wanted to desperately marry her. When the King came to know of his son's silly infatuation, he was furious. He threatened the Crown Prince that he would never be allowed to become the King if he did not forget the peasant girl. It was then the Crown Prince proudly declared:

'I, the Crown Prince, do hereby abdicate my crown for the sake of my love.'

'Never show me your face again!' the King thundered and he repudiated the Prince.

So the Prince gave up his crown, princely robes, sword and horse and walked out of the palace. Never had he felt so free in his life!

The ex-Crown Prince went to meet his ladylove on foot. Sans his crown, regal robes and majestic white horse, the girl's father did not recognize him.

'Who are you?' he demanded

'Why! I am the Crown Prince! Well...I should say I was the Crown Prince. The King would never allow me to marry your daughter. So I gave up my Crown for the sake of my love. So here I am, free to marry your daughter!' the Prince proudly said.

'And pray, what makes you feel I will give my daughter's hand in marriage to you, O! penniless Prince!' mocked the man.

The prince was taken aback but he was sure that his ladylove would not jilt him.

'Let your daughter decide that,' the prince said confidently.

The man called for his daughter. When she came she was surprised to see the Prince dressed like a peasant and enquired what had happened. She was disappointed to learn that he was no longer a Prince.

'I was in love with the Prince, not you,' she 'decided' abruptly; she had no second thoughts.

The Prince was stunned and he had to leave with a heavy heart. He realised that he had made a fool of him. He could not go back to the palace and if he continued to roam about in the kingdom, he would become a laughing stock. So he fled to a neighbouring kingdom.

At first he was too proud to do any menial job or to beg. After all he had been a Prince once. But his hunger soon got the better of his pride and he began to do odd jobs. He had no previous experience in doing these jobs. Hence he could never do a job to the satisfaction of his employer and he was always mocked at. The only job he had been comfortable with was that of a prince and he had lost it forever.

Whenever he received a verbal stab, his glorious past would catch up with him and he would whisper: 'Once I was a Prince.' Whenever he looked at his shadow it seemed to be decked in princely robes and crown and then in shock he would look at himself, only to find that his clothes were ragged and torn. When he slept, he was haunted by dreams of his erstwhile princely life and would mumble in his sleep: 'Once I was a Prince.' Gradually he lost his mind.

One day he was squatting on the pavement, as if in a trance. A passerby mistaking him to be a beggar dropped a coin for him. The Prince looked up and with a stupid smile on his lips, said:

'Once I was a Prince.'

'True, but now you are a beggar,' the man replied with a contemptuous smile

'Once I was a Prince,' the beggar repeated.

ONCE I WAS A PRINCE – A Discussion

Richard said, 'I think the Prince is symbolic of many organizations that refuse to turnaround; they refuse to change because they live in a constant state of denial.'

'Very true, it is very difficult to conquer denial. A turnaround would depend upon how fast an organization changes its stand from 'that can't be true!' to 'things have changed, so let us change'.' Anne agreed

'And why do organizations refuse to change?' Richard asked 'It is often because of their glorious past. As Rosabeth Moss Kanter points out, the past success often creates a 'halo effect' which hides their weaknesses and glorifies their strengths. Their products thus become desirable. So long as he was the Prince, the Prince was desirable and the moment he ceased to be a Prince, his lady love jilted him. And the Prince never recovers from this shock. So he becomes passive.'

'And passivity and a feeling of helplessness bring about a bankruptcy in ideas. Instead of taking initiative, he feels that he can do little to make a difference in his fortunes. So he becomes a pauper. The days of monarchy and autocracy are over for him and instead of learning to do things by himself he laments the loss of the only job he was comfortable with – that of the Prince.' Anne said.

'But how does a company actually effect a turnaround?' asked Richard.

'I think it will be worthwhile to examine Nissan's turnaround, under the stewardship of Carlos Goshn.' Sterling said. 'Perhaps Goshn's biggest challenge was overcoming the deep denial inside Nissan about the company's precarious condition. People inside thought that the *kieretsu* which is a Japanese network of permanent financial, human and business relationships would come to its rescue; if not the bank, then the government would rush to his rescue. But the brutal reality was that such insider bonds had been severely affected by a decade of economic stagnation. Realizing this, Goshn entangled Nissan from the *kieretsu* and he then set up cross-functional teams that were empowered to uncover any problem and set challenging yet realistic goals. He eliminated 21,000 jobs, closed five factories, increased funding for research and introduced new models. Today he has driven Nissan to eleven per cent operating margin. But the key to the revival was abandoning the *kieretsu*.'

'So, never sit still and let future happen – change and change again.' Sterling said. 'The past, especially when it is glorious, is desperately captivating. It often haunts and distorts the present to such an extent that we become myopic to reality. And slowly the past takes complete charge of our lives. Unless we break out of this infantilizing past and show that we are in charge, we will never be able to change. In a constantly evolving environment, one needs to continually change to remain relevant.'

'Today, for example, we have no job security and hence we should develop portable skills that will make us employable, always.' Anne said.

'So I think we need to become 'possibilitarians',' Richard said. 'We must be extremely adaptable to cope with changes that do not occur by choice but are forced upon us by circumstances. You can either be a creature of circumstances or bend circumstances to your will.'

'Forget the past, live the present, love the future.' Sterling concluded

9 | The Five Guardians

'The Five Guardians have come! The Five Guardians have come!' shouted little Pancho excitedly as he ran through the narrow lanes of the village. Pancho was the grandson of Sanchez, the village Chieftain. Perhaps Sanchez had thought that little Pancho was the best person to communicate the good news, as he was a bundle of vibrant energy with the shrillest vocal chords.

Out of their little huts, the villagers emerged, their faces now radiating a newfound hope and curiosity, to see the 'Five Guardians'. Soon there was a huge crowd outside Sanchez's house; each man, woman and child were vying with each other to catch a glimpse of the five men who would deliver them from the evil Sancho Paza and his band of bandits, who had been ravaging the village with impunity for many years.

The villagers had approached the Governor many times and the Governor had sent his soldiers to defend the village. But whenever they saw the cloud of dust raised by Sancho Paza and his bandits approaching on horses, they would tremble like leaves and even before they reached the village, they would flee. A few times the soldiers had claimed to raid the hills where Sancho Paza and his men would retire. And they would always return stating their search was in vain.

It was then one of the gypsies visiting the village told them about the Five Guardians. They were a wandering band of mercenaries who had successfully guarded villages against notorious bandits. Before leaving the village they would train the villagers to defend themselves against any future attacks. They charged a hefty fee for their services but then the fee was fully justifiable.

The presence of the Guardians drew comments and sighs of admiration from the motley crowd. They were all tall, well-built, handsome men in their forties with long hair and their faces were brimming with confidence. The maidens of the village were known for their beauty and each of them had fallen instantly in love with the five men; they couldn't help sighing; their hearts were fluttering with the question whether they were married.

One of the Guardians lifted a cute little girl to his shoulders and began to play with her. This naturally drew another round of sighs.

Sanchez cleared his throat and thundered in his hoarse voice.

'My dear fellow villagers, didn't I promise you that I would bring the Five Guardians to save our village. So here they are…. the…Five…. Guardians!' Sanchez announced dramatically laying emphasis on each word.

There was a thunderous applause from the crowd.

'Amigos! Our friends have traveled a long way. I would request the heads of any five families to give them accommodation.'

The moment he had finished saying these words, there was almost a riot among the men to do the honour of playing the host. Finally the fortunate five households who would play hosts to the Five Guardians had to be decided by drawing lots.

So the Five Guardians slept, bathed and ate and by evening they were practising and the whole village watched them. Then they planned how to erect barricades to check the bandits and the villagers carried out their instructions. The arrangements were completed late in the night. That night the villagers slept peacefully after praying that nothing untoward should happen to the Five Guardians.

They were woken up in the wee hours of the day by the sound of heavy fighting. Earlier someone would keep watch on the tower and would warn the villagers when the bandits approached. The warning would only help them to be ready to face the onslaught by seeking shelter in their homes.

They witnessed the Five Guardians in full flow; they were giving Sancho and his men a very hard time. Sancho had twenty men of which the Five Guardians had already killed three. The bandits were facing such skilled swordsmen for the first time and were completely caught unawares. Seven more men fell in quick succession. That was too much for Sancho. For the first time in his life he uttered, 'Retreat!'

And the bandits were waiting for that direction. It was a pleasant sight for the villagers to see the bandits fleeing for their lives.

The villagers lifted their saviors on their shoulders and began a procession of victory through the village. Two of the Guardians were wounded but their wounds were not serious. However the maidens nursed their wounds seriously.

'I don't think Sancho will ever dare to return to this village. Villagers! On your behalf I thank these gallant men for saving our village from the clutches of the vicious Sancho Paza. It was a pleasant sight to see those rouges beating a hasty retreat. I couldn't help laughing. Ha! Ha! Now let us celebrate,' bellowed Sanchez.

'I don't think the time is ripe for celebrations, my good men. Sancho will return for revenge. I feel we should take this battle to his den and complete it there,' one of the Guardians said.

The other Guardians nodded.

'But you are wounded!' the maidens said with deep concern.

'Oh! These wounds are not serious,' replied the amused Guardians.

One old woman stepped forward and with folded hands requested thus:

'Oh! Gallant Guardians, if you are going to Sancho's hideout, will you not rescue our daughters who were taken away forcibly by the cruel Sancho. I don't even know whether they are even alive.' And then she began to cry.

One of the Guardians embraced her and reassured her.

After resting for some time, they started their arduous journey to the hills. There was no one to guide them, since no one had dared to even go near the hills. As they went deeper into the hills they drew their swords ready to counter any surprise attack. Then they heard excited voices. It was Sancho Paza and his men talking.

'We must attack the village this night... we will torch every hut in the village!' Sancho Paza was heard grunting.

'We have already lost ten of our brothers and now you want us to lose our lives?' one of his men shot back.

There was silence for some time

'I make the decisions here... if anyone is not willing to follow me I will execute him now!' thundered Sancho Paza.

'That will make our task easier, Sancho Paza,' one of the Guardians said as he entered the hideout.

The startled bandits looked around them; the Five Guardians were walking towards them from five directions. One of them made a desperate dash towards the group of ladies whom they had forcibly taken from the village; perhaps he had thought that the only way they could escape was to threaten to kill the ladies if the Guardians did not give up but he was stopped mid way by a dagger thrown at his neck by one of the Guardians. Two of the Guardians encircled the ladies to protect them while the others clashed their swords with the bandits. One by one the Guardians struck the bandits down dead and finally only Sancho Paza was left behind. Sancho was the only person who could offer some résistance as he was a good swordsman but in the end he found his sword thrown away from his hands and the tip of the Guardian's sword at his neck.

'We are going to take you to the village; let the villagers decide what is to be done with you,' said one of the Guardians.

Sancho Paza smiled slyly and then suddenly pulled the tip of the sword at his neck through the neck and he dropped dead.

'The Five Guardians have returned and they have brought back our daughters!' shouted the man at the watchtower at the top of his voice.

Little Pancho heard the man shouting and carried the news running from one hut to another like a bumblebee, repeating like a parrot what he had heard. The villagers ran towards the main gate to welcome the Guardians and their long lost daughters, with Sanchez at the forefront waiting with open arms.

'Welcome back! Gallant Guardians! And welcome back dear daughters! Oh! Gallant Guardians I do not know how to thank you…. The whole village is grateful to you....I ....I,' he stammered and then he broke down, choked by emotion and cried like a little child.

Many of the ladies and the men, who were on the verge of crying, now burst out into tears. They had cried like this many times but that was when Sancho Paza either killed or maimed or usurped their kith and kin. The mentally strong also now made an attempt to cry as they felt they had to co-operate in this collective effort; perhaps they felt that this was their last chance to cry in the foreseeable future. Not knowing what their parents were crying for, the little children also began to wail. It looked like a competition to cry, which reached a high pitch when the long lost daughters were reunited with their mothers.

Even the Guardians were deeply moved and there were tears in their eyes.

Finally Sanchez pulled himself together and raised his hand in a gesture to stop crying and like the orchestra that wound up on seeing the last flourish of the wand by the composer, the crying stopped!

'Its time to celebrate!' Sanchez declared.

And so the village celebrated and celebrated like it had never done before. The maidens waited impatiently for a chance to dance with the Guardians.

'This seems the perfect place to settle down,' sighed one of the Guardians, his eyes meeting the admiring gaze of a beautiful maiden.

'The best food, the best wine. ...and the most beautiful damsels I have ever seen,' another Guardian agreed.

'A pity that we have to leave this place after training the villagers,' sighed another

Then one of the Guardians had an idea; he said, 'What if we don't train them.... then we can live here for ever.'

'What do you mean?', the other Guardians asked.

'What I have in mind is this – we will waive our fee in return for staying in this village... forever. But we will never fully train the villagers for if we train them we will lose our importance,' the Guardian who had come up with the idea said.

'I am sure that would be an offer the village will not refuse,' the other Guardians agreed.

The next day the Guardians were making their way to meet Sanchez to tell him of their offer. The old woman who had cried and begged the Guardians to bring back her daughter when they had set out in search of the bandits, made an extempore exhibition of crying, bettering her previous performance. She had started her performance the moment she saw the Guardians coming and she was squinting at the Guardian who had consoled her at that time.

'Who will marry my daughter? Who will marry a woman who has been forcibly taken by bandits and lived with them?' she wailed.

The Guardian turned back and said, 'I will!'

'Oh! Thank you! Thank you! God will certainly bless you!' cried the old woman, tears flooding her eyes.

'That's magnanimous of you!' said Sanchez, 'But there is only one problem – those who marry the girls of our village must settle down in our village by tradition. But since you are a wandering warrior we can think of making an exception…'

'No! No! I am willing to settle down here!' the Guardian said abruptly. 'In fact we all wish to settle here for ever.'

And then the Guardians told Sanchez about their offer.

'There cannot be a greater joy for us than you staying with us. But you must teach us to defend ourselves. Sancho Paza is dead but that doesn't mean that we have seen the last of the bandits,' said Sanchez.

'I don't think anyone will dare to think of becoming a bandit so long as the Guardians are with us,' said one of the villagers.

'So long as the Guardians are with us …but what happens after that? What about the future? You just seem to be interested in living each day as it comes,' Sanchez rebuked him.

'Sanchez is right,' one of the Guardians said, 'we will teach you how to defend yourselves but in return you must teach us something which we do not know'

'And what is that?' the villagers asked.

'Farming!' said the Guardian and he began to laugh.

All the villagers began to laugh but Sanchez did not find that amusing.

'I mean if we are to settle here, we must learn farming… to make a living,' the Guardian said sensing Sanchez was not quite effusive.

So the villagers taught the Guardians farming but the Guardians did not teach them warfare. And the villagers did not care to learn. Sanchez kept on reminding the villagers but soon he found that the villagers were treating him like a nuisance. Hence he stopped advising and limited himself to shaking his head in disapproval, which in turn stopped with his death a few years after.

The Guardians became good farmers.

The last of the Guardians was being laid to rest and little Pancho who was the headman now was giving an impressive speech. (He was still little in stature, though not little when it came to age; he was now forty)

While he was giving his speech, he was continually distracted by his little son, who seem to be paying little attention to his speech and was staring at something. Finally he interrupted his father, pointing his finger at the horizon.

'Father, is that a storm approaching?' he asked.

All eyes turned to that direction.

A cloud of dust was steadily approaching the village; the cloud of dust soon turned into twenty horsemen who were now firing their guns and shouting.

Little Pancho gave the only possible order he could give as the Village Chieftain.

'Bandits! Run for your lives!'

THE FIVE GUARDIANS – A Discussion

'Sancho's concern is very relevant – 'So long as the Guardians are with us …… but what happens after that?' Anne said 'But in good times, such critics are rarely listened to. What this parable brings to my mind is the need for succession planning; about creating leaders for tomorrow to take care of the future.'

'Very true, Anne!' Richard said. 'Leaders are not infallible. Hence Leadership has to be collective and pervasive. It is the summation of every little act, every little decision taken by each employee of a company. Hence it is very important to empower each employee first with information and then with resources. So what we need is not a Lone Ranger or a five man army but a village equipped to fight the bandits.'

'It is difficult to retain talent and it is often more difficult to maintain the wisdom of the talent that leaves the organization.' Richard continued. 'That underlines the need to institutionalize the wisdom in the organization. In my organization, I make it a point to ensure that anyone who goes for a learning program shares that learning with his colleagues. Secondly, I believe that for all levels, at least three people should be groomed for succession.'

'That's good, Richard, but not good enough.' Sterling said. 'Have you found your successor? I mean, you are the owner of your company. Even those companies that nurture successors to middle level managers often fail to keep ready a pool of potential candidates for the CEO job. There must be a robust process to identify at least two to five CEO candidates and develop them and when I say develop, their on the job experience and their education must be completely aligned to the emerging landscape. The Board and the current CEO must own responsibility for this. A case in point is how Jack Welch identified twenty potential candidates and later narrowed it down to three.'

'Thanks, Sterling.' Richard said. 'That's real food for thought! And the first thing I am going to do when I get back to my company is to set a CEO succession plan in motion.'

10 | The White Elephant

Milano knew how to make money and also how to squander it. He was an astute businessman always alert to pounce on any opportunity to make a decent profit and that way he made a lot of money. But he had two weaknesses that ensured that he wasted money as fast as he earned it. One was gambling and the other, buying anything that would appeal to him in a bizarre way.

There would be times when he would almost be penniless. But then he would bounce back seizing some business opportunity that rained him a windfall of profits. His wife, Sylvia, had put up with him through his erratic fortunes and eccentricities, although she continually nagged him.

Business reasons and wanderlust often took Milano to strange lands. There he would come across exotic animals and things and he couldn't resist buying them, even at exorbitant prices, only to be greeted by a barrage of curses from his wife, on his return.

But this time he knew he had gone too far.

He had bought a white elephant! And that had necessitated employing the mahout also.

When he reached home, his wife was at first relieved to find that Milano had not brought any quaint object with him. But her relief was short-lived as she heard the trumpet of an elephant; at first she thought she had imagined hearing it. Then she came out and saw a white elephant in the compound and she almost fainted.

'Oh God! How much did you pay for this... white. ...elephant?' she shrieked.

'Fif...fifty thousand gold coins,' Milano stammered and to justify what he had done meekly added, 'Isn't he majestic?'

'Fifty thousand! O Mialno! You are really out of your mind!' Sylvia screamed.

'Dear wife... give me a chance to explain. Have anyone of us seen a white elephant before? Imagine people staring at us in wonder and envy as we ride on this elephant in the streets. This white elephant will enhance our prestige. It is said that a white elephant will bring a lot of good luck; my business will prosper hundredfold. He is certainly the most exotic and majestic object I have ever bought. So I think he is worth fifty thousand gold coins,' Milano said.

'You and your insane ideas! I will not ride this elephant and make a mockery of myself!' Sylvia said as sharply as she could, stamping her feet in disapproval.

That night, Milano was too excited to sleep; he could hardly wait to have a ride on his elephant through the streets.

The next day morning, when the streets were full of people, Milano made a dramatic appearance, perched proudly on his white elephant. As the elephant strode majestically through the streets, the people were stopped in their tracks; they stared at this exotic animal with their mouths wide open. Milano was amused by the startled expression he saw on their faces and he was pleased with himself.

That day his house swarmed with friends and well-wishers; there were persons who he had never met before but they all seemed keen to scrape acquaintance with him. They wanted to take a closer look at the white elephant and begged for a ride on it. Milano was only happy to oblige.

Then came the priests from the temple; they wanted the white elephant to lead the grand procession that would mark the end of the annual festival. Milano felt flattered. In a single day he had become the most famous person in the city and he owed all this to the white elephant.

The next day, the King summoned Milano to his palace; he had graced the annual procession with his presence, the day before and Milano had noticed that he was very impressed with the white elephant.

It has to be something about the white elephant, thought Milano

'Milano, your white elephant is truly a majestic animal, something that a King would be proud to possess,' the King said

'Thank you, your majesty,' Milano said.

'I want to buy your white elephant; I will pay you one hundred thousand gold coins.' the King said.

Milano thought for a moment and then replied: 'Your majesty has made a magnanimous offer. But I have an emotional attachment to the articles and animals I have come to possess over these years; especially to this white elephant. I hope you will be kind enough to understand my position if I say the white elephant is not for sale.'

'Very well then, let us leave it at that,' the King said.

When Sylvia learned about the King's offer, she was furious.

'How could you refuse such an offer? It was a golden opportunity to get rid of that animal,' she said.

'I will never sell my white elephant!' declared Milano indignantly.

Maintaining a white elephant was an expensive affair as Milano was to realize and he was not deriving any tangible benefits from it. Almost everyone in the city had hitched a free ride on the white elephant and it had now become a familiar sight in the city. Also it did not bring any luck in his business as he had expected. In fact he had lost a lot of money through gambling.

The initial euphoria gave way to stark reality.

Gradually he reached a stage where he could not feed the white elephant.

'If you cannot afford to feed it, then you must either sell it or allow it to starve and die,' Sylvia doled out another unsolicited advice.

And for the first time in his life, he felt like heeding her advice.

The next day, Milano met the King.

'Your majesty, I wish to sell the white elephant to you,' Milano said.

'What about emotional attachment?' the King teased

'Nothing is emotionally stimulating than money, your majesty', Milano replied with a smile.

'Very well, I offer twenty five thousand gold coins for the elephant.'

Milano was stunned by this offer; he had to at least recoup the money he had spent!

'Your majesty, you had previously offered me one hundred thousand gold coins'

'Now my emotional need to own a white elephant has scaled down. You can take my offer or leave it,' the King replied sarcastically.

The King had turned out to be a shrewd customer; he had perceived that Milano was desperately in need of money and hence he knew he could drive a hard bargain.

So, finally Milano sold the white elephant to the King for half the price he had bought it.

But he was relieved to get rid of the animal. Now it was the King's headache as long as he could afford to feed it.

THE WHITE ELEPHANT – A Discussion

'Like Milano, we throw good money after bad even when we know it is a dud investment. I wonder what dissuades us from divestment even in such a case.' Anne asked.

'I think it is due to the fear that even when we realize that the investment is a failure, that we might sell it for too little – what if it proves a great buy to the acquirer and more important, the very fact that there is a buyer makes you feel that it is not bad after all. We would rather spend some more money to complete an unviable project than write it off.' Richard said.

'I feel we must be prepared to kill strategic experiments at the earliest once we realize that they are not viable. Companies are often used to making big bets. And some of these bets do pay off but if they fail, they make a heavy dent on the bottom line and may sound the death knell of the company. What do you think, Sterling?' Anne asked.

'What I feel is that you can make a larger number of small bets; they are more likely to lead to a larger number of breakthrough innovations. Companies like Whirlpool have already proved this.' Sterling said.

'I am also reminded of how some celebrities spent their money on many snobbish investments which they later find difficult to maintain.' Sterling continued. 'Pet projects and personal ambitions often put tremendous strain on one's resources. If they are not delivering the results, one needs to emotionally detach oneself from such projects and shelve them. But that is easier said than done because no one will give up a cherished belief and your stubbornness stands in the way of accepting that you have made a mistake.'

11 | The Two Princes

King Valerius hid behind a huge tree.

His minister looked at him, baffled.

'Your Majesty, why are you hiding behind this tree?' he asked.

'Shh!' whispered King Valerius, placing his finger on his lips and rolling his eyes, 'Be patient! The princes can come out any moment.'

The minister was still confused. *Was the King going to spy on the princes? And why would he do that?* He thought.

The princes and their classmates came out, led by their tutor. The tutor gave swords to the elder prince, Prince Xerxes and one of his classmates and asked them to give a display.

The two young men bowed before their tutor and commenced the duel.

Within a few moments it was clear that Prince Xerxes was gaining the upper hand.

'Look at the way he fights, your majesty!' whispered the Minister excitedly.

King Valerius was filled with pride when he saw his son wield the sword so deftly.

The opponent was disarmed in no time.

Prince Xerxes in a fit of excitement suddenly rushed to the opponent, raising his sword to strike. King Valerius' heart stopped for a moment; he was about to rush out from his hiding and stop the prince when the tutor intervened timely. Even when the teacher held his hand, the prince was trying to jerk off his hand.

The King and his Minister saw the teacher rebuke Prince Xerxes; it was then the prince dropped the sword and came to his senses.

Next, it was the turn of the younger prince, Prince Darius.

Prince Darius wielded the sword with such effortlessness and grace that the King was impressed. But he soon began to wonder whether the grace would do him any good as the opponent seemed to be gaining on him. It was clear that this was a worthy adversary; it was not going to be a one sided battle as witnessed before.

'Your Majesty, I feel Prince Darius is going to lose this duel,' whispered the Minister.

King Valerius stared at the Minister in disagreement.

But Prince Darius maintained his composure and just when everyone thought the fight would come to an end with his opponent emerging victorious, he disarmed the opponent, leaving him spellbound.

Then Prince Darius dropped his sword and embraced his opponent. Even the tough King Valerius was moved by this gesture.

King Valerius saw the teacher patting the back of the prince and advising the disciples about something and the King instantly understood the teacher was asking the students to emulate the prince.

King Valerius and his Minister exchanged meaningful glances. The Minister noticed that there was a look of relief on the King's face – it was as if he had finally found an answer to the question that had been harrowing him for a few months.

Ten days from now, he would declare who his successor would be. If he were to follow tradition he would not have been in any doubt, he just had to declare Prince Xerxes his successor. But then, King Valerius did not believe in tradition, which was not supported by reason.

He had been receiving reports regarding the progress of education of his two sons from their tutor. In terms of warfare and academics the princes were equally good. But the tutor had opined that Darius was more level headed.

To King Valerius, when it came to choosing the next King, it was character that mattered most.

The day for coronation of the crown prince arrived. The palace was filled to the brim with expectant courtiers. Prince Xerxes and his circle of friends were visibly excited. There was murmur in the palace, which died instantly when King Valerius got up.

The King surveyed the crowd and said:

'Dear Citizens, I have had the honor of being your king for many, many years. All these years I have been in relentless pursuit of glory and fame and it's my ardent belief that I have brought glory and fame to my kingdom. But now I am tired. I wish to embrace asceticism and go in search of peace. Hence I feel the time has come to declare my successor,' King Valerius paused and then continued.

'Years ago a King defied tradition by choosing the youngest of his four sons as his successor and that was me. In doing so he was guided by reason and not tradition. The decision I am going to make is also guided by the same principles and keeping in mind the welfare of my people.'

All eyes now watched the King's lips.

'I hereby declare... Darius as my successor,' he declared

There was a collective sigh from the crowd; Prince Xerxes stared at the King as if a bolt from the blue had struck him; Prince Darius looked around him nervously when he realized that he was now the cynosure of all eyes.

'Come...Darius.' King Valerius invited him.

Prince Darius bowed before the King and the Queen and ascended the throne. Then the King took the crown from his head and placed it on Darius's head.

A few months later, King Valerius embraced asceticism and left the kingdom.

During this time, one of the powerful states refused to pay the taxes and declared it a separate kingdom.

Xerxes offered to quell the rebellion. Darius was moved by this gesture and agreed.

A few weeks later, a soldier who was in Xerxes's army came to the court and presented a harp to King Darius – the harp was Darius's favourite musical instrument.

'Your excellency, I have a message from Prince Xerxes,' he said.

'Read out the message, my good man.' Darius said.

'Greetings! King Darius the Great! I am sending a harp to you, which I am sure you will love. After all, your soft hands are capable of only playing the strings of a harp; they are unworthy of holding even a sword. My dear King! I have joined forces with the very state you have sent me to annex and I am marching towards my kingdom. If you receive me at the main entrance singing paeans with this harp and place the crown on my head, which rightfully belongs to me, I will spare your life; you can spend the rest of your life singing and begging. If not,

I will chop off that undeserving head of yours and take the crown myself!' the soldier read out.

For a few moments, there was a deafening silence and King Darius's face reflected every pang of shock and betrayal he felt. He then gestured his tutor to follow him to the chambers.

'What must I do?' he asked.

'Do? Do what any king would have done – send a fitting reply to your brother, marshal your forces and deliver a humiliating defeat which will force anyone to think twice before he revolts against you,' the tutor said without any element of doubt.

'But he is my brother and by tradition this crown rightfully belongs to him,' Darius said.

'Your father placed the crown on your head because he was convinced that you would make a better ruler than your brother and to this day you have proved him right. Please do not allow your heart to rule your head; the kingdom is in need of a good ruler; not a good brother.' There was steel in the tutor's voice, this time.

'The hands that play the harp so deftly must be equally capable of wielding the sword when the occasion demands,' he added

When the words of his tutor sank in, anxiety vanished from Darius's face and it radiated supreme self-confidence.

When he reentered the court, he took the harp his brother had sent him and began to pull out the strings one by one and when the last string had been undone, he handed over the string – less harp to the messenger and said: 'Tell my brother that the hands that are capable of playing the strings of the harp are also capable of plucking them out too. Tell him if he dares to attack me, his condition will that be of this string-less harp!'

Darius's words sent a chill to everyone in the court.

Xerxes stood before Darius, his head hung in shame- shame from the humiliating defeat he had suffered; he had never expected to be defeated. The image of the harp without the strings loomed in his mind. To his left was Carlyle, a notorious robber and murderer who had murdered seven men, three women and two children.

It was Darius's birthday and according to tradition, the King would pardon one criminal on his birthday.

Will King Darius pardon Prince Xerxes or Carlyle? That was the question everyone had in mind.

All eyes turned to King Darius who seemed lost in thought. The conversation he had with his mother in the chambers a while ago was reverberating in his mind.

'Darius, pardon Xerxes, I beg you. He is after all your brother,' she had begged.

'Mother, he is guilty of treason and the penalty for treason is death,' he had replied.

'But you are the king; you can make or break rules. Punish him if you want, imprison him... imprison him for life... or... banish him but please don't execute him,' his mother had begged him again.

King Darius set aside his thoughts and pulled himself together; everyone leaned forward listening intently.

'Take Carlyle to the gallows; I don't see any reason why I should forgive a person who usurped twelve lives including two children. So, the death penalty stays,' he declared.

Xerxes and the Queen breathed a sigh of relief – if Carlyle was to be put to death, it would naturally follow that Darius would pardon Xerxes; tradition demanded that he free one prisoner on his birthday.

'Henceforth I will not pardon any prisoner on my birthday. Once a judgment is made, it stays; the guilty are to be punished and not to be pardoned; why should I pardon someone just because it is my birthday?' Darius said.

So I have the dubious distinction of being the last criminal to be pardoned. He will probably banish me, thought Xerxes

'Xerxes, I find you guilty of treason and there is only one penalty for treason – death! Take him to the gallows and behead him!' Darius passed the sentence as if he was addressing an ordinary citizen.

The Queen fainted and the soldiers began to drag Xerxes away. Xerxes was at first too shocked to protest. When he managed to find his voice he begged for the first time in his life – for his own life.

'Your majesty, I beg you, please don't execute me. Banish me! Imprison me! But please don't behead me! I am your brother!' he cried

'I will never make a good ruler if I break the rule to save my brother. The hands that play the harp must be equally capable of wielding the sword when the occasion demands. Soldiers! Do your duty.' King Darius ordered.

Some incidents in this story are based on the life of King Samudra Gupta

THE TWO PRINCES – A Discussion

'I feel the parable is about egalitarianism – about treating everyone with equal respect. And believe me it is a very tough thing to do. Among other things, it means being 'firm and fair' and fairness means the ability to deal with the facts of the case rather than considering the person involved.' Anne gushed 'But ,' she continued, 'I am proud to be part of a company that not only preaches but practices egalitarianism. We have a policy that expressly prohibits any form of unlawful employee harassment based on race, colour, religion, sex, national origin or age disability. Each employee has the responsibility of maintaining a workplace that respects differences, values and diversity and thrives because of their common objectives.'

'The policy was put to test when one of our star employees was asked to leave when charges of sexual harassment was proved against him. The company proved that it valued and respected women; in this case the woman employee in question was of a lower designation. Also in our culture, no perks are conferred on select employees. It is a culture of equals.'

'In the recent past, we have seen that many high profile

CEOs have had to go. They were given marching orders by the Board because the Board felt that these executives did not live up to the very high standards of the posts they held. I believe this is a step in the right direction since its will ensure better governance' Sterling said.

Their eyes turned to Richard who seemed to be lost in thought.

'Richard?' asked Sterling.

'I am glad, Sterling, that I could take part in this discussion,' Richard said, 'I have always treated people according to their rank or title and conferred perks on select employees. Now I realize that I have to create a culture of equals where the executive vice president and the janitor are treated with equal respect.'

'Anyone can be polite to a king, but it takes a gentleman to be polite to a beggar.' Anne said

'I'll remember that, Anne. I am also impressed by the way the King chose his successor putting reason above tradition. I find in it very relevant in a legacy company like mine where the challenge will be to transfer leadership from the generation of owners to the next generation. And I am not going to forget about succession planning which we discussed under 'The Five Guardians'.

12 | The Dramatist

The play was over. Penworth looked anxiously at the faces of the spectators. There was no response from them for a few moments. He could not make out from their faces whether they were moved or disappointed. He had presented a tragedy and it was a tragedy of epic proportions. Generally plays presented were comedies and when they were not comedies, they at least had a happy ending. But his play had been bold, realistic and true to life but the pertinent question that now loomed in his mind was whether the audience was prepared to appreciate and accept it.

His father, who was the court dramatist, had confessed that he had liked the play but would not endorse the same, as he knew that the King would not like to watch a tragedy.

The King got up from his seat slowly (in his prime he would have got up abruptly) and began to applaud furiously pausing once or twice to wipe his tears. Then the Crown Prince got up and applauded; he too was seen wiping his eyes though there were no tears in his eyes. Then the whole audience got up to its feet and the applause became thunderous.

Each applause sent strokes of thrill and pride through Penworth's veins.

The King gestured Penworth to come near.

'Gentlemen, Penworth has taken us through an overwhelming emotional experience which is true to life. May his tribe increase!' said the King

The King then gave his necklace to Penworth. The Prince hurriedly pulled out one of his rings and gave to Penworth.

'Great play! Penworth, Great play!' he said

The King looked at the Prince with contempt.

Penworth bowed before them and then looked at his father who seemed on the verge of breaking out into tears. He went to his father and embraced him.

'You have proved me wrong, my son!' he said 'The King has never praised any artist so much! I am sure you will be made the court dramatist in no time.'

The King and the Prince left the hall. While they were walking, the Prince asked the King.

'Your majesty, what was so great about that play?'

The King stopped and regarded the Prince for sometime.

'Then why did you say the play was great and give your ring?' the King asked.

'Since you gave him a necklace I had to give him a ring!' the Prince said

The King shook his head and said, 'Next time you part with your ring, convince yourself that the recipient is worthy of the honour.'

The Prince looked baffled.

'Are you saying that Penworth was not worthy of the honour?' he asked

'He certainly deserved the honour but you were not convinced whether he deserved the honour,' the King said.

The play was over. Penworth did not look anxiously at the faces of the spectators, for he knew he would get a standing ovation this time too; he had presented a better play this time. There was no response from them for a few moments. All eyes turned to the King and Penworth's eyes too turned with anticipation to the King. The King smiled at Penworth and said something. From the movement of the lips Penworth could make out that he said 'Good!'

The Prince got up and began applauding. He said excitedly, 'Great Play! Great Play!'

Then he removed one of his rings and gave to Penworth who bowed with gratitude as he received the gift. All the time the King was staring at the Prince with anger; then as hurriedly as old age would permit him, he left the hall with the staff in his hand. The Prince ran to catch up with him.

The Dramatist

'Why did you leave the hall in such a hurry without congratulating Penworth? Wasn't it another great play?' he asked.

The King stopped and again regarded the Prince for some time. Then he spoke, 'Yes, it was a great play when viewed in isolation but I don't think it measures up to his first play. In many ways it resembled the first play and anyone could guess the ending. And I don't think it is a great idea to pat Penworth on the back every time he comes up with a play. In fact I wanted to talk to him in private about what I felt; it was then you gifted him a ring... again!'

'But I think it is my duty to encourage him!' the Prince protested.

'My dear Prince, if you really want to nurture talent, then your praise should be inconsistent. Otherwise it will be merely flattery and flattery is the easiest way to kill talent!' the King said.

The Prince still didn't seem to understand. The King shook his head and walked away.

Penworth wondered why the Prince had summoned him.

'Penworth, by now you might have come to know that I am in love with Lady Camlin.'

The Prince said

'Your majesty, she is indeed fortunate to be chosen to be the wife of the greatest Prince in the world!' Penworth said.

'However ... there is a problem.'

'Ah! What problem could possibly be there?'

'I feel she is in love with my cousin.'

'Your cousin! I... I don't understand. Why, you are at least ten nay hundred times worthier than he!'

'Yes, I know. But there is one art in which, I must admit, he is stronger than I am and that is poetry and Lady Camlin simply loves poetry. That's where you come in.'

'How can I be of service to you?'

'I am impressed by the passion you display in the verses in your play. I want you to use all your creative faculties to write the most passionate and beautiful love poems ever written and then you must teach me how to recite them passionately to my ladylove. Of course, I will have to claim that I wrote them and why not, in one way, haven't I inspired you to create them?' the Prince said.

After a pause he continued, 'And if I win the heart of my ladylove, I will do everything in my power to make you the Court Playwright.'

Penworth's eyes lit up.

'But I understand that the King is in favour of Sir Wordsell; after all he is senior to me,' he said

'Forget about seniority; it is talent that matters. And I am sure that you are the best talent available in the kingdom. As I told you before, I am impressed by the passion displayed in your verses,' the Prince assured him

'Ah! Your majesty was kind enough to gift me your ring but the King was not impressed.'

'Oh! I am sure he was. But you know he is getting old; maybe he didn't want to part with one of his jewelry. Penworth, put your fears to rest. Remember, I am the next King!'

The High Priest placed the crown on the Prince's head. The Prince, now the King, looked at Princess Camlin (now Queen Camlin) and smiled at her.

'Please observe silence for a few moments in memory of my great father,' the King said

After a few moments, when all the courtiers had settled down in their chairs, the King got up.

'The post of the Court Playwright has remained vacant for quite some time,' he said.

All eyes now turned to Sir Wordsell. But Penworth had a sly smile on his lips.

'I hereby appoint Sir Penworth as the Court Playwright,' declared the King.

There was a stunned silence in the court.

Sir Balmore, an Earl whispered to the King, 'Your Majesty, I think you have made a mistake. Sir Wordsell has proved himself to be the greatest playwright of his times through his thirty plays. Penworth... has just written two plays. Besides, Sir Wordsell is twice the age of Penworth. Please reconsider your decision.'

'Sir Penworth is more talented than Sir Wordsell and I count talent more than gray hairs,' the King said with a sneer.

The play was in progress. This was Penworth's fifth play and he was sure that once the play was over he would receive the fifth ring, the fifth pat on the back from the King, the stale words 'Great Play! Great Play!' would spout from the regal mouth for the fifth time and there would be a standing ovation for the fourth time (since he had missed one when the old King was the guest of honor) and why not?

Now the King was involved even in the writing of the plays, he would suggest the plot, the characters, the opening, the climax.... everything except the verses which thankfully he could not pen and when the play was declared before the audience the King was mentioned as a co-author.

But the King had to leave midway since he got an urgent message that his father-in-law was sick. But the play continued as it was specially staged in honour of the King of the neighbouring kingdom. Before leaving, the King handed over something to his neighbour and whispered something in his ears.

The audience now grew restless; some of them started yawning; the others began to fall asleep. They would not dare to do that in front of the King, as they knew that Penworth was the favourite of the King.

Then Sir Balmore got up and left the hall. Soon the nobles began to leave the hall, one by one. By the time the play was over, everyone except the King of the neighbouring country and the guards had left.

Penworth bowed before the guest of honour. The guest of honour was snoring soundly. The guards gently woke him up. He got up from his seat abruptly as if he had been woken up from a nightmare.

'The King asked me to give this to you,' he said and he handed over one ring to Penworth after rubbing his eyes.

Penworth bowed before him and turned to go. Then the guest of honour suddenly remembered something and spoke thus:

'Oh! One more thing, Great play! Great play! Come near to me, Penworth; let me pat your back'.

THE DRAMATIST – A Discussion

'People always live up to our expectation of them or live down to them, whatever the case may be,' said Richard. 'If you don't expect much from your employees, they will sense that and perform poorly because it is your expectation that affects their desire to do well. In this parable, we find the dramatist living down to the expectation of the Prince; he knows whatever trash he may turn out, he will get a praise, a pat at the back, a standing ovation and a ring. We need to move from good to great and from great to exceptional and for that we need to continually upgrade our expectations and communicate our expectations clearly.'

'Anne?' asked Sterling.

'Recognition and praise are of course two things people want more than sex and money,' said Anne, 'But a pat at the back has to be at the right time and not every time. As the King advised the Prince, 'make sure the recipient is worthy of the honour'. One shouldn't make promises of rewards the main reason for employees to perform; rewards are recognition of a job well done and not simply the goal of doing the work. It all boils down to rewarding right.'

'A pat at the back at the right time always motivates a person. But what if he is constantly patted? Praise to be effective has to be specific; otherwise it is flattery and flattery kills talent. I will conclude by quoting Norman Vincent Peale:-

'The trouble with most of us is that we would rather be ruined by praise than be saved by criticism.' Sterling said.

13 | The Knight and the Farmer

William's eyes gleamed with pride as he watched his elder son, Uther to plough the field.

He said to his wife: 'Here is a dutiful son who listens to his parents and works hard. I will make him the best farmer in this village. How I wish his younger brother were like him!'

His eyes were suddenly filled with worry and dismay when he mentioned his younger son and he sighed deeply.

'He wants to be a soldier,' his wife said haltingly.

The farmer's expression now turned to contempt.

'Soldier! Soldier!' he repeated as if the soldiers' profession was the lowest he could think of. 'Why doesn't he think of becoming a farmer like his brother?' He gesticulated irritatingly.

He sighed once again and looked up at his wife; she was trying to avoid eye contact.

The Knight and the Farmer

'Martha, do you want him to be a soldier?' he asked

'No! Never! That's the last thing I want him to be,' Martha said

It was mid day and Uther returned from the fields to have his lunch.

'Where is Ector?' he asked

'Out to watch the joust,' Martha said scornfully

It was then Ector rushed in; he was visibly excited.

'Look at what I have made!' he shouted displaying proudly two wooden swords.

'Yes, look at what your son has made. Aren't they great?' William said with scorn.

'Not only can I make them I can also wield them,' Ector said confidently brandishing the sword with a flourish.

'You should have strong arms to hold the sword,' Uther said with a slight smile on his lips.

'So you doubt my strength! I challenge you, Sir Uther, to a duel! Here is your sword,'

Ector shouted as he hurled his sword to Uther and charged towards him. Ector brandished his sword as if he were fighting for his life while Uther fended with mock seriousness. In a few moments, Ector disarmed Uther and pointed his wooden sword at Uther's throat.

'Surrender or die!' he shouted

'All right, all right, I surrender. Thou art the finest swordsman in the whole of the country,' Uther scoffed at Ector, as he bowed in mock reverence before him.

The duel though conducted with wooden swords had taken away the breath of William and Martha.

'Ector! Put down the sword at this very instant!' William shouted.

'Oh, father, this is just a wooden sword!' laughed Ector

'Even with a wooden sword you were fighting as if you were possessed! I wonder what you would have done had it been a real sword... you even forgot it was your own brother standing there!' rebuked Martha.

'This was a mock duel!' Ector protested

'True, this was a mock duel. But in a battle, you will have to face a skilled enemy who will stop at nothing short of beheading you,' William said

'I can measure up to any enemy; all I need is some training; how many times have I begged you to request Sir Kent to take me as a page?' Ector shouted.

'So you are still hell-bent on becoming a soldier?' Martha asked.

'Yes! Yes! Yes!' Ector said adamantly as he stomped his feet and then he stormed out of the house.

'Adamant, undutiful son!' cursed William

Martha's shock had now crystallized into tears.

'Now, mother, don't cry. I know where he has gone to. Let us leave him alone for a while. Then I will speak to him but I don't think I can change his mind,' Uther said.

Ector sat cross-legged on the shores, his eyes scanning the vast sea. This was the place he frequented whenever he had a fight with the members of his family.

He suddenly felt a hand on his shoulder and he looked up; it was Uther.

Uther sat beside Ector and looked at him; his gaze was still fixed on the sea.

'Ector, I will persuade father to speak to Sir Kent,' said Uther

'You will?' asked Ector, his eyes lighting up.

'Provided....'

'Provided.... What?'

'Provided you convince me why you want to be a soldier; in other words why you don't want to be a framer.'

'Why I want to be a soldier? First of all it's not a mere soldier that I want to be; I want to be a knight. A knight defends his country, wins battles and brings glory to his country. Right now, we are building an empire; our country is in need of soldiers. And if you prove your mettle you can rise in ranks and even become an Earl. Think of the power and esteem that an Earl commands! On the other hand if you are a farmer, you will remain a farmer throughout your life.... there is no progress.... I mean there is no 'Lord Farmer'. Is there?' Ector replied passionately.

'And who feeds the soldiers who bring glory and who feeds the country?' Uther said sharply.

'But a farmer will never get recognition. Look at Sir Ellis who hailed from our village who went on to become an Earl. How did he become an Earl? He was our father's neighbour but each time he passed father's way, father would bow before him to pay respect. Father has put in fifty years of toil as a farmer but has he received any appreciation or recognition even from our village? Sir Ellis served only a few years under our king and today the whole country treats him with awe.' Ector said

'But your father has outlived him. You know that Sir Ellis was killed in the battle when he was barely forty. Ector, all it takes to put an end to that glorious life that you have been talking so eloquently about is for an arrow to find the right place in the armour' argued Uther.

'Men like Sir Ellis never die; their supreme sacrifice immortalizes them. And besides who wants to live forever! I would rather die in the battlefield than spend rest of my life confined to this wretched farm and die as an obscure farmer. Now have I convinced you?'

The Knight and the Farmer

'And what about Claire?' Uther asked knowing that this was the last arrow in his quiver.

For once Ector faltered. 'Well...what about her?'

'Her father would never approve your joining the army which means you will never be able to marry her.'

'If that is the price I have to pay to realize my dream, then.... I am willing to do so. But I am sure she will wait for me.'

'I have nothing more to say, Ector' Uther said sadly, shaking his head.

So Ector joined as a page under Sir Kent. He soon became the favourite of Sir Kent and was made a squire. That year he got his first opportunity to take part in a battle.

Two ladies in the village prayed fervently for Ector's safety – one was Martha and the other was Claire, who was adamant that she would marry only 'Sir Ector'.

By now, William had retired from work and was enjoying a peaceful life, with the farm entrusted in the safe hands of Uther.

Uther married and had one child and each year he became a better farmer.

One day as Uther was tilling the field; he noticed a cloud of dust fast approaching – it was a knight on a horseback. As the knight came near, he drew his sword. Uther looked around him – there was no one but him on the field. He realized with horror that the knight was charging furiously towards him. His instinct told him he was about to be killed by the knight and he took to his heels wondering what he had done to invite the wrath of this knight.

The knight broke out into a fit of uncontrollable laughter and Uther turned back as the voice was very familiar to him. The knight dismounted and lifted his visor and Uther saw a face wreathed in smiles – a face that he had been missing for quite some time – that of Ector.... Or.... Sir Ector?

'Ector! You really took my breath away! For a moment I thought...' said Uther stopping intermittently to catch his breath.

'You thought you were going to be killed? O brother! I never knew you could run so fast. In fact, you ran faster than our enemies when we routed them,' Ector said, laughing in between.

'The fastest sprint a man runs in his life is when he runs for his life. Anyway have you ... become...a...'

Ector did not allow Uther to complete.

'A knight? Yes Sire! You are now speaking to Sir Ector!'

Uther knelt solemnly before Sir Ector and in a voice choked in emotion, said 'You are the first knight in the family.'

Ector was moved and he warmly embraced Uther. As he

did so, he could see with his moist eyes, his mother running towards him.

'Ector, my son! At last, you have come home safely. God has answered my prayers!' she cried as she hugged him tightly as though she had missed him for decades, her eyes flooded with tears.

'Mother, your son has become a knight!' Ector announced proudly. But Martha continued to hug and kiss Ector as though her hearing was impaired.

Ector shook her gently and repeated what he had said earlier; this time saying each word slowly and emphatically as though he was teaching a child to repeat what he said.

'Yes, I heard you. Knight, Earl or farmer, you are my son first and I am worried only about your safety as any mother would be.' said Martha.

Ector was at once disappointed and moved; disappointed because his mother just didn't seem excited about his knighthood and moved because her love and concern for him was overwhelming.

Sensing Ector's disappointment, Martha said, 'I am of course proud that my son has become a knight.'

'Where is father?' Ector asked.

'He has gone to take part in the village fair; he will be back by lunch,' Martha said.

'In that case I will go and meet someone and return by lunch,' Ector said.

'Why don't you tell your own mother that that 'someone' is Claire.'? Martha said, laughing.

The brave knight blushed scarlet.

'You may now kiss the bride.' The priest said

Sir Ector kissed Claire for the first time.... before the entire village.

And then he sighed – a sigh of relief, satisfaction, pride.... that comes with achievement... when dreams come true. All his dreams had come true... no... he had realized his dreams.

He looked at his parents and his brother and remembered vividly how they had dissuaded him from becoming a knight. He chuckled within himself when he remembered the look of disbelief in his father's eyes when he saw.... no... when realization dawned on him that his son had become a knight. He had returned from the village fair, eager to share with his wife and elder son what he saw and did at the fair when Uther startled him by announcing dramatically.

'Father, a knight has come to join us for lunch!'

The next morning he had caught Uther wearing his knight's armour and regarding himself before the mirror and challenging his reflection to a duel.

That day Claire's father had visited his house for the first time in many years and that too to give his daughter's hand in marriage to Sir Ector; all his protests had melted away the moment he heard Ector had become a knight!

So many things had happened in that one day!

Sir Ector once again looked at his family and relatives.... they were farmers...simple, obscure farmers yesterday but today they were the kin of Sir Ector!

Yet there was one thing he couldn't understand.

He had asked his family to leave the farm and come and live with him in his manor but they still wanted to stay in the farm.... it was as if they had resigned themselves to the fact that they would spend the rest of their lives in that wretched obscure farm.

But he had to move on.... move on from the farm to the manor; move on from a mere knight to an Earl.

William, Martha and Uther continued to live in their farm as before.

The only change that happened to their lives was that they came to be known as the kin of Sir Ector.

Then Sir Ector's country declared war on a neighbouring country; the two nations were equally powerful and hence war meant a long and protracted war that would last decades.

Claire was pregnant when Sir Ector left.

During the first year of Ector's campaign, William died and Claire gave birth to a son but Ector could not come home.

Three years after, Martha died; Ector still could not come home.

And year after year, Uther became a better farmer, a better father, and a better husband after having already proved that he was a dutiful son. But then to quote Sir Ector's words: 'There is no 'Lord Farmer'…. is there?'

It took five more years for Ector to come home.

Uther was working in the field when a knight came, riding on a white stallion, with a staff with the national flag fluttering proudly in the wind.

The knight dismounted and lifted his visor. It was not Ector.

'An arrow has found the right place in my armour.' Sir Ector said to Uther with a sad smile on his lips; his eyes now turned to Claire and his son who were weeping.

He had hoped to see his brother, one last time and hence had dispatched his friend to bring his brother. They had won the war; he had fought valiantly. But he would not become an Earl.

He clutched the hands of Claire and Uther tightly and then sighed – a sigh that comes with the realization that there is nothing more that can be done. He then looked at his five-year-old son; his gaze was fixed on his son for a few moments. Then the tightness with which he gripped the hands of Claire and Uther ebbed away.

Sir Ector was twenty-nine years and three hundred days old when he died.

Among the heroes who had made the highest sacrifice, Sir Ector's name was also counted.

Uther lived for another fifty years – long enough to see his children grow and marry and rear their children. And when he died, he was the best farmer, the best husband, the best uncle and the best grand father in the village but it was as the brother of Sir Ector, the villagers remembered him

THE KNIGHT AND THE FARMER – A Discussion

'I could easily identify with Ector,' 'Richard said. 'Here is a guy who is passionate about living his dreams. When I ventured out of my family's business, I invited a lot of criticism from my parents and brothers. They wanted me to stay with the family business. They felt that there are only limited opportunities in any other area. But I believe that there are no limited opportunities, only limited imagination. And in business, a family that stays together to do the same kind of business need not grow together.'

'But there is always a high price attached to all this success – a price called stress' Anne argued. 'One coveted thing that most people lack is peace of mind. As Uther points out all that is needed to undo all that success is for 'an arrow to find the right place in your armour'.

'But then there is no 'Lord Farmer' is there?' Richard countered 'You need to take chances. All that Uther achieved was becoming the best farmer in the village but he was remembered as Ector's brother.'

'I think it boils down to one question,' Sterling said 'How

would you like to be remembered? What is your legacy? And then you have to work back. Both Ector and Uther are right in their own ways – both became the best in what they were good at. And don't we need both farmers and soldiers? Find a distinct positioning for yourself consistent with the kind of person you are and what you are good at. Remember what Booker. T. Washington said, 'No race can prosper till it learns that there is as much dignity in tilling the field as in writing a poem."

'And let us not forget what John F. Kennedy said.' Anne added. 'I don't mind if my son chooses drilling roads as his occupation, but he should be the best at that'.

14 | A War Averted

The General of the Kingdom of Neece blew out an irritated, impatient breath. He had been waiting for his King's orders to march to the Kingdom of Hail.

When he first heard the news, he was astounded – the Queen of Neece had been missing!

Only two days before, the King of Hail had arrived in Neece. The purpose of his visit (so he had claimed!) was to explore new opportunities for trade between the two kingdoms.

The King of Hail was known to be a notorious womanizer; he was also incredibly handsome. The Queen of Neece was a ravishing beauty who would employ all her wiles to seduce the man she desired; kings had waged bloody wars to court her favour.

Any kingdom would desire to have trade with Hail as it was a prosperous kingdom. The two kings were to sign a treaty that would open the gates of trade between the two nations and the day the treaty was to be signed, the King of Hail had disappeared quietly!

It was as clear as the day that the Queen of Neece had eloped with the King of Hail!

It was a black, shameful day for Neece.

War with Hail was now a certainty; it was an age when even petty bickering escalated into protracted wars. Hence the General had put his army on alert. But strangely, the King was still procrastinating and it puzzled the General.

Finally the King summoned the General.

The King sat glum faced in his throne, his right arm cradling his chin.

'Your majesty, we await your orders to march to Hail,' the General said

'We are not marching to Hail,' mumbled the King.

For a moment the General thought he had heard the King wrong, but when the courtiers began to exchange shocked glances and speak in muffled voices, it suggested otherwise.

'I beg you pardon, your majesty,' the General said

'You heard it right, General; we are not marching to Hail,' the King reiterated and this time he was explicitly clear.

'But why, your majesty?' the General persisted.

'Why should I wage a war for the sake of a woman who

no longer loves me?' asked the King.

'But it is a blow to our pride and this insult must be avenged!' the General protested.

'You are being sentimental, General and Sentiment is the mother of War,' the King said. After a pause, he added, 'And Sense is the mother of Peace.'

The General wondered for a moment since when this monarch had turned into a philosopher. All the courtiers seemed to share his thought.

The King felt he owed his court a further explanation.

'I know you are intrigued by my decision but I have given serious thought to it. Let us say we declare war on Hail. Winter will set in any time and many of our soldiers will die on the way. The army of Hail is equally mighty and the war will certainly go down in the annals of history as the longest and the bloodiest war ever fought. And at the end of the war, which will take decades, we will have two impoverished nations, which at the beginning of the war were wealthy, and a hag who at the beginning of the war was a serpentine beauty. And what do I do with her? Parade her through the streets and execute her for her infidelity? When the pains of war clearly outweigh its gains, it must never be waged!' he said.

'Now tell me, is it worth waging such a senseless war for the sake of an unfaithful spouse?' the King asked.

The General felt uncomfortable when he realized that the

question was hurled at him. He looked around and found that all eyes were on him.

'No, your majesty,' he replied without thinking any further; he felt stifled and wanted to leave.

Sensing his discomfiture, the King said 'Very well, General, you may leave.'

The General hastily left the court.

The King's glance fell on his younger brother who seemed to be visibly disappointed. He had hoped that the King would entrust him with the affairs of the state and lead the army to Hail. He had always coveted the throne but was afraid of conspiring against his powerful brother.

If the war had broken out, he could have been the King for decades. And there was always a chance that the King might get killed in the war. And if that did not happen, he could conspire to get him killed and declare himself the King.

But the King's decision had torched his ambitions.

A smile appeared on the King' face – it seemed he had read his brother's mind.

A WAR AVERTED – A Discussion

'What inspired you to write this parable?' Anne asked.

'The Trojan war', replied Sterling, 'I mean that war was waged for a single woman – Helen of Troy. If you look at the wars fought, most of them have been fought either for personal glory or for beautiful women. They rarely made any sense to the people.'

'I think the King is a very level headed, practical person who clearly weighs the 'pains and gains' before taking a decision.' Anne said. 'Emotional stability or consistency in moods is something which I don't often find in many leaders. Often their decisions and what they say are distorted by their emotions and mood swings.'

'In other words, Emotional Intelligence' Richard said. 'It is emotional intelligence that helped the King to make a rational behavioural choice. Business decisions are often guided by short-term gains. Personal ambition, sentiments and emotions often blur and distort long term vision and stand in the way of taking decisions in the interest of the organization.'

'Richard, do you feel Emotional Intelligence is the

triumph of head over heart?' Sterling asked.

'Is it not so, at least in this case?' Richard asked.

'I beg to differ.' Sterling said. 'It is neither the triumph of head over heart nor the heart over head; it is the intersection of both. The King uses his emotion to assist thinking and then uses that thinking to analyze his emotions. So he is aware of his emotions and acts on his emotions in a rational way.'

'Hmm... I get it. Be aware of your emotions and accept your emotions; do not suppress them or bottle them up. But before succumbing to our instincts and emotions we must ask as the king asked 'Is it worth it?' Sterling said.

JAICO PUBLISHING HOUSE
Elevate Your Life. Transform Your World.

ESTABLISHED IN 1946, Jaico Publishing House is home to world-transforming authors such as Sri Sri Paramahansa Yogananda, Osho, The Dalai Lama, Sri Sri Ravi Shankar, Robin Sharma, Deepak Chopra, Jack Canfield, Eknath Easwaran, Devdutt Pattanaik, Khushwant Singh, John Maxwell, Brian Tracy and Stephen Hawking.

Our late founder Mr. Jaman Shah first established Jaico as a book distribution company. Sensing that independence was around the corner, he aptly named his company Jaico ('Jai' means victory in Hindi). In order to service the significant demand for affordable books in a developing nation, Mr. Shah initiated Jaico's own publications. Jaico was India's first publisher of paperback books in the English language.

While self-help, religion and philosophy, mind/body/spirit, and business titles form the cornerstone of our non-fiction list, we publish an exciting range of travel, current affairs, biography, and popular science books as well. Our renewed focus on popular fiction is evident in our new titles by a host of fresh young talent from India and abroad. Jaico's recently established Translations Division translates selected English content into nine regional languages.

Jaico's Higher Education Division (HED) is recognized for its student-friendly textbooks in Business Management and Engineering which are in use countrywide.

In addition to being a publisher and distributor of its own titles, Jaico is a major national distributor of books of leading international and Indian publishers. With its headquarters in Mumbai, Jaico has branches and sales offices in Ahmedabad, Bangalore, Bhopal, Bhubaneswar, Chennai, Delhi, Hyderabad, Kolkata and Lucknow.

SINCE 1946

www.ingramcontent.com/pod-product-compliance
Lightning Source LLC
LaVergne TN
LVHW091306080426
835510LV00007B/387